DATE DUE			MAY 29 '73
DEC 1 5 2000			

How You Can Make Big Profits Investing in Coins

HARRY J. FORMAN

Former President, United Coin Collectors Alliance
Life Member, American Numismatic Association
Member, Professional Numismatists Guild
Member, American Association of Appraisers
President, Harry J. Forman, Inc.
P. O. Box 5756, Philadelphia, Pa. 19120

NUMMUS PRESS

New York

Published by Nummus Press
Box 1058, Flushing, New York 11355

Copyright © Harry J. Forman, 1972

Library of Congress Catalog Number 77-174309

ISBN 0-87841-002-3

Printed in the United States of America

Contents

Introduction

Anyone can make predictions, and if he does so in a field in which he is already well known, they are sure to be widely read. Moreover, by waiting until people's memories have become somewhat blurred, and then republishing only his successes, he can often build up a rather good reputation for himself.

In the numismatic field we have three different kinds of forecasters. The first and commonest is the person who makes predictions simply as a promotional device to help sell whatever he has on hand. I don't say that in all, or even most cases, this involves a deliberate deception. On the contrary, the very fact that a person has invested his own money to purchase one or another item would indicate a certain amount of faith in its market potential. But such predictions necessarily lack true discrimination, and depend for their success, if not on luck, then on the progress of the market as a whole.

A second type of forecaster is the non-professional numismatist who dabbles in speculation and writes books or articles on market trends. Such an individual is more serious in his selections, and understands that there are always widespread differences in the potential of various issues' and series.' But for all that, his livelihood is not dependent on his predictions, and even should they fail he is still reimbursed by his royalties.

The third and rarest type is the successful full-time dealer who forecasts not for promotional purposes, but simply to share his insights with the general investing public. My good friend Q. David Bowers is one such forecaster, having given much excellent investing advice through the *Empire Review* and more recently the *Rare Coin Review*. I am likewise a forecaster of this type, and my published predictions on U.S. coins can be checked by anyone who has access to the back issues of *Numismatic Scrapbook Magazine*. However, as many of you will be new to the field, I am going to make things a little easier by publishing herewith a complete list of those predictions. This, in fact, is the least any genuine prognosticator owes to his audience. If his record is so poor that such a disclosure would prove embarrassing, then, in my opinion, he ought to turn to some other vocation.

My own recommendations began with the February, 1958 issue of the *Scrapbook*. At that time I offered to "dealers with foresight" a number of silver dollar rolls (i.e. twenty silver dollars) which I felt were very much undervalued. Here are the issues, the prices at which I sold them, and the prices for which *single specimens* were being advertised in 1964.

	My Roll Price, 1958	Single Coin Price, 1964
1880-CC	$47.00	$55.00
1881-CC	42.00	75.00
1882-CC	32.00	22.00
1883-CC	32.00	22.50
1884-CC	32.00	40.00
1885-CC	43.00	70.00

Suppose you had been one of those who followed my advice and purchased the above six rolls in 1958. For your $225.00 expenditure you would today have coins worth $4,700.00!

In the October, 1958 *Scrapbook* I specifically recommended the eleven piece set of silver nickels (1942-45), an item I have continued to bring to people's attention, and which, even at the present time, I consider a good investment. For one thing, these are the only twentieth century five-cent pieces to have silver in their composition. For another, they are unique among Philadelphia Mint coins in that they bear a mintmark.

When, in 1956, I first started selling these sets (and, incidentally, I was the first person to do so), I felt they were important enough to merit a special container. Accordingly, and in anticipation of future demand, I had made up 10,000 custom holders, and it is from the depletion of these that I can exactly count my early orders. My initial price, container included, was only three dollars, and the reader should remember this figure when, in a little while, we return to the subject of these sets.

In my 1958 ad, I offered the silver-nickel coins as rolls, that is forty each of the eleven issues. The price was a then modest $85.00. True to my expectation, the set began to climb at a fantastic pace. By the end of 1959, it was being quoted at $360.00, an increase of over 400%!

In December, 1958, I added a number of new predictions, the first involving the 1955-S cent roll. I stated that this item, which was then selling for about $5.00 would, within a year, be worth double that figure. When the time came around, it had in fact climbed to $9.75 and was being sold by some dealers at no less than $11.00. I also predicted that the 1955-S dime, 1955-D quarter and 1955-P half dollar rolls would show nice gains over the same period. As it turned out, the dimes increased from $6.50 to $15.50, the quarters from $14.00 to $19.75, and the halves from $12.85 to $16.25. Again, I said that the 1939-D nickel, which was then selling for about $12.50 per coin, would in a year's time reach $20.00. As a matter of fact, it did much better than that. As of December, 1959, the coin had virtually vanished from the market, and dealers were offering to *buy* specimens at $28.75 each, *in roll quantity!*

The remainder of the predictions made at that time were general, relating to such series' as the modern denominations, earlier uncirculated coins, proof sets and U.S. gold. In all these areas, the market continued to show the gains I expected.

In March, 1960, I listed a large number of coins which I considered sleepers and which, if bought at that time, would show handsome profits in the future. Since I set no time limit, it will not be unfair to compare the prices at which I then sold them to those attained during the 1963-64 peak period.

Item (All B.U. Rolls)		Price I Sold it at in March 1960	Price Attained During 1963-64
1¢	1934	$ 47.50	$170.00
	1934-D	150.00	600.00
	1935-D	37.50	175.00
	1935-S	65.00	285.00
	1936	20.00	35.00
	1936-D	22.00	120.00
	1936-S	32.50	180.00
	1938	38.00	75.00
	1938-S	42.50	215.00
	1939-D	100.00	275.00
	1942-S	45.00	212.50
	1943	11.00	12.50
	1943-S	37.50	55.00
	1955-S	9.00	40.00
5¢	1942-I	25.00	107.50
	1942-S	50.00	167.50
	1944-D	40.00	82.50
	1946-S	22.00	78.00
	1950	67.50	193.50
	1950-D	225.00	925.00
	1955	47.50	145.00
10¢	1955	37.50	127.50
	1955-D	35.00	75.00
	1955-S	23.50	67.50
25¢	1952-S	45.00	130.00
50¢	1950-D	65.00	195.00
	1953	35.00	230.00

Just imagine if you had been one of the lucky persons who followed my recommendations and then sold your holdings at their peak prices.

In January, 1962, I advertised a special group of items, accompanying each with the price at which I believed it would be selling a year hence. For example, I offered silver and gold commemorative type sets at $1,600. and $1,650., respectively, predicting that each of these would be worth over $2,000. As it turned out, the silver set reached $2,500., and the gold $2,100. I also offered an about uncirculated 1955 double die cent for $105., forecasting an increase of about 50%. At the end of a year this coin had actually doubled in value and, of course, no one was complaining about the bonus.

I offered rolls of 1960 small date cents for $135.00 each, suggesting that they would go over $200.00. And here occurred one of those amusing quirks of fate which, to this day, collectors discuss with relish. At the end of the year, this roll had reached only $155., and those who liked to talk about my infallibility were not a little chagrined. Should they sell, they asked? By no means, I insisted. For I knew my coin, and wasn't about to let a few months rob me of my prediction. Accordingly, the faithful held onto the roll, and, lo and behold, by the end of the year it shot up to no less than $395.00. It had made good with a vengeance.

The next item I offered was the 1950-D nickel roll. The price was $230., and the prediction was that it would at least reach a $300. level. By the end of the stipulated period, it was actually selling for $400.00.

Perhaps the least successful of my forecasts involved the 1948-D half dollar roll. I had offered it at $25. and predicted its rise to the $40. level. It did indeed reach and even somewhat surpass this figure, but its arrival was about nine months late.

As usual in the course of my predictions, I called attention to the silver nickels. In this particular ad I offered sets of single coins at the still low price of $10.00 each, predicting a 50% rise by the following January. As it turned out, the set didn't begin to move until March, 1963. However, in the ensuing months it more than made up for this procrastination. By June, it was being traded at $17.50 and within six months of that time it had climbed to $42.50. Now recall that only seven years before, I was selling this same set for a mere $3.00. When, at that time, I predicted its rosy future there were not a few who smiled. It was now my turn to smile, and of course the turn of all those who had followed my lead.

In the final prediction made at that time, I said that $20.00 gold pieces, which were then selling at a mere $47.50, would eventually return to and even exceed their all-time (1947) high of $70.00. As of the present year, this had been fulfilled.

In January, 1963, I made a list of new predictions which I offered free to anyone who would contribute a dollar or more to the Lewis Reagan memorial foundation for the betterment of numismatics. Needless to say, I was swamped with requests. Unfortunately, this list was never published, and I no longer have a copy of it. However, in the September, 1963 *Scrapbook* I made reference to three of the predictions and so can at least report these. The first was for the 1950-D nickel roll which I said would reach the $500. mark within twelve months. As of September, it had already risen to the $700. level. Secondly, I predicted that the 1947-S nickel roll would be worth over $50., and it was now up to $60.00. Finally, I recommended the 1960 proof set with the small date cent. At the time of the prediction it was selling for a mere $18.50, but as of September it already exceeded the $40. level.

I should also mention my April, 1963 ad wherein I recommended the investment potential of ten New Orleans mint silver dollars (from 1890 to 1904) which I was offering for $54.50. By the end of 1964, these same coins were selling for about $84.00.

There it is my friends, and to the best of my knowledge a complete listing of my published predictions of U.S. coins. Whether you grade it 90%, 100% or 200% correct, you must admit that the leads were well worth following.

The reader may wonder why, after such unusual success, I suspended my predictions in 1964. The reason is that the Mint had already unveiled its plan to discourage roll collecting by removing the identifying characteristics of the various issues. There were some who failed to read the meaning of these words and continued to forecast a rosy picture for the future of modern U.S. coins. One well known investment counselor even predicted that the 1950-D nickel roll would climb to $10,000! My own views were much less optimistic for I suspected that, at the first sign of trouble, the many new speculators who had pumped big money into rolls would immediately bolt, starting an irreversible downward trend. And so it happened.

Today, after its long purgation, the modern U.S. coin market is starting to regain its health, and, like many other areas of numismatics, offers a fertile field for investment. Because of this and also the many requests that I resume forecasting, I have undertaken the present work. My aim has been to cover not only the modern issues, but all areas of American numismatics, and, in a summary fashion at least, the foreign market also. If in these uncertain times I have assisted would-be investors in finding a fertile market for their hard-earned money, I shall feel more than compensated for my labors.

H.J.F.

August 1, 1971

Chapter 1
How You Can Profit with Silver Coins

Throughout history there have been many periods in which a people watched helplessly while the purchasing power of their money dwindled down to a fraction of its original worth. Such financial crises have come to virtually every nation at some time or another, our own not excepted.

These crises are not as a rule built up overnight, but develop from the cumulative result of various government decisions and internal circumstances. In our own country we can look back to the years 1933-34 as the period when the first seeds were sown for our present hard times. It was then, you may recall, that our gold coinage was demonitized, gold bullion nationalized, and gold itself revalued from $20.67 to $35.00 a troy ounce. This meant that the dollar, silver and paper, was suddenly devalued by some 40%, though, domestically, it did not at the time seem to affect anyone but numismatists, whose collecting of gold coins was for many years restricted.

But gold demonetization had two very bad effects. First, it permitted the Government to issue as much paper currency as it pleased without fear of any runs on its gold reserves by its own citizens. To be specific, it resulted in an increase of our money supply from $39 billion, just before World War II, to the present $214+ billion. In the process, it assured us not only of a steady inflation, but, ironically, of the gradual erosion of U.S. gold reserves due to redemption of our overseas dollars by foreign nations.

Secondly, the retirement of a precious metal which, throughout history, had served as a standard of value in commercial dealings set a very bad precedent. It led, in 1965, to the retirement of silver from the coinage (except for a token amount in the 1965-70 half dollars) and then, which was far worse, to the demonetization of silver certificates. Heretofore, it had still been possible to obtain silver granules for the value of these notes, but now the Government said in effect: "It is wrong for you to require us to back our paper with something of genuine value. We are the greatest producer in the world and our currency can never fail."

Thus, in little more than a generation, the money of the American people changed from a healthy bimetallism to a fiat paper currency without any backing whatever. Now I would be the last person to argue that bi-metallism is a perfect system, or even practicable in our present day and age. But it seems that governments, like people, never know when to stop, and so, on retiring gold and silver coins, just can't resist the temptation to do away with the backing of the paper money. And this despite the obvious fact (for all history is a lesson) that fiat currency can only result in continual inflation and financial losses for its citizens.

Down through the ages, whenever such financial crises threatened, prudent citizens have always sought to protect themselves by investing in various items which were expected, relatively speaking, to maintain their value. Among such items, objects of art and coins have figured prominently.

Whenever the subject of inflation hedges is discussed, there is usually some mention of "diversification." There is certainly nothing wrong with this, but it requires that you become adept in not one but several fields, which is time consuming when accomplished, and dangerous when it is not. Again, there is an element of uncertainty when investing, say, in paintings done by an unknown artist. This is especially true at the present time when art criticism seems to be at low ebb. I am reminded of the several occasions when paintings done by a chimpanzee have been entered in competitions and done quite well. Imagine buying thousands of dollars worth of paintings only to discover that the artist was an ape! This, of course, is an extreme case, but even when the artist is quite human there is no guarantee that he is ever going to become famous and his works valuable. Of course, you can start out by only buying the works of famous names, but then you must be prepared for a very large cash outlay. Works of art are also relatively bulky and fragile, which is why, in addition to the above, I prefer a straight investment in coins.

So we'll agree for argument's sake (and it really is a good argument) to collect coins. But what precisely should we collect? If we're new to the field, haven't much time for education and are basically conservative, the best thing I can suggest is bags of silver coins. There are some very sound reasons behind this advice, but before I spell them out, I'd like to make the field a little more attractive by telling you something about the history of our silver coinage and its manipulation for private profit.

Though silver coins were struck at the Mint as early as 1794, their successful circulation (except for half dollars) was long prevented by various factors. In the case of the dollars, their heavy weight (and thus excessive value) caused them to be exported to the West Indies for recoinage into the lighter Spanish pieces of eight. The latter were then sent to the U.S. Mint for melting and recoinage into dollars—a lucrative if not altogether patriotic practice.

The smaller denominations, i.e. quarter dollar, dime and half dime also had their troubles, in this case because of the wide circulation of small Spanish silver coins in the country. The latter were generally so worn that it was unprofitable either to melt them down for industrial use, send them to the Mint for recoinage, or, again, to export them as bullion. Thus, in accordance with Gresham's law, they drove out the "good money," or rather, in this instance, kept it from ever being minted. Even after three decades, there was still less than one quarter dollar, dime and half dime (taken collectively) for every person in the United States!

After this time and until 1849, our silver coins fared a little better, but with the California gold rush, the value of silver began to climb and the coins were again exported. In 1853, a law was passed reducing the weight of the silver coins (except for the dollar), and this would have been a very sound measure had Treasury officials not mismanaged the distribution of the coins. As it turned out, they were issued in far larger quantities than could be absorbed, and soon clogged the channels of trade.

Then, with the Civil War and the issue of our first federal paper currency, coins of all kinds once more disappeared from circulation. The silver denominations were not seen again for fifteen years, that is, until the Comstock Lode bonanzas and a coinciding depreciation of silver in Europe combined to bring them to a parity with the greenbacks. Finally—you guessed it—the coins returned in such quantities that they were a nuisance for fifteen years.

Something more should be said about the silver dollar. I have already described how the earliest issues were being exported to the West Indies for conversion into pieces of eight. This situation continued until 1804, when the dollar denomination was suspended. It was reinstated in 1840, and all went well until the gold rush and consequent rise in the value of silver. Unlike the subsidiary coins, the weight of the silver dollar was not reduced, a concession, as it turned out, to the silver bullion dealers who were complaining bitterly about the curtailment of their private enterprise. Thus, silver dollars continued to be exported and were never seen in domestic circulation, which is why their demonetization in 1873 passed unopposed at the time. It was only after the passage of a couple years, when the price of silver had begun to drop, that the western mining interests got so upset and demanded a resumption. They lobbied vigorously for the free coinage of silver, by which they hoped to bring 371¼ grains of the metal to the Mint and, regardless of its market value, receive a dollar in exchange. In short, they wanted to play the bullion dealers' game! In 1878, a compromise was reached whereby the Government agreed to purchase silver for coinage into dollars—but only at the prevailing market price.

The Bland-Allison act, which provided for the resumption of the cartwheels, authorized the Mint to coin between two and four million dollars worth of the coins each month. The quantity was far greater than could be circulated, and soon the coins were gathering dust in the Treasury vaults. As if this weren't enough, the silver interests continued to press for the free coinage of their metal despite the fact that it was continually declining in value.

By mid-1890, there were some three hundred million silver dollars kicking around the Treasury Department, 82% of the entire amount coined since 1878. Congress now passed a remedial act, or so it imagined, which authorized the further coinage of dollars from silver purchased by the Government with treasury notes. Secretary Windom unwisely gave in to public demand for redemption of the notes in gold, and this led to a sudden tremendous rush on our gold reserves. By 1893, the situation had become critical, and the silver purchase clause was repealed. But silver dollars continued to be coined, at least until 1904, by which time the silver lobby had sustained some major political defeats.

Then, in 1918, a curious circumstance triggered renewed demands for silver dollar coinage. During the World War, the price of silver had risen to nearly its old parity with a dollar's worth of gold, causing a severe shortage of the metal in British India. Great Britain appealed to the U.S., who, had it been free of partisan interests, would simply have melted down the millions of dollars in its vaults and sold the bullion. But at this critical juncture, the silver interests again became vocal and brought about the Pittman Act of April 23, 1918. This act provided not only for the melting and subsequent sale of up to 350,000,000 silver dollars, but also that the Government purchase an equal amount of bullion from American mine owners and strike new dollars for all those melted down! The result, of course, was our Peace dollars, which were issued from 1921 to 1935.

During 1964, renewed pressure from the silver producers temporarily prevailed on President Johnson, but at the eleventh hour he rescinded his own order for resumption of dollar coinage. Now, in the present year, the latest chapter of this interesting denomination has just unfolded with the coinage of Eisenhower dollars. Three different issue are projected, viz. 40% silver proofs, 40% silver non-proofs, and clad cupro-nickel.

Such, in brief, is the history of our silver coinage, and if I have emphasized the major roles played by bullion dealers and mining lobbies, it is only with the purpose of pointing out that such traffic is an old and accepted tradition in the United States.

Perhaps the best reasons I can give for an *immediate* investment in silver coins is that 1) they can still be purchased at close to their face value, and 2) with the inevitable increase in the long-range value of silver, their own value can only go up.

There have been various conflicting opinions with regard to the future of silver, but of one thing there seems to be little doubt—

namely that shallow, high-value ore deposits are gradually drying up. This means that the cost of labor to extract silver will continue to climb and in turn require an upward valuation of the metal. Even at the present time, only about one third of the world's silver production derives from direct mining, the rest originating as a by-product of lead, copper and zinc. A time must therefore come when the available supply of the metal, which is so much needed by the photographic and electronics industries, becomes critically low; and this in turn can only result in a dramatic increase in its price.

Now let's go back a few years and see precisely what has been happening in the uncertain world of silver. Prior to World War II, there seems to have been no shortage of the metal, and, as of 1941, its mean value on the New York Exchange was only $.351 an ounce. (Whenever we speak of gold or silver ounces, we refer to the troy ounce of which twelve equal an avoirdupois pound.) However, as in the case of World War I, the war years brought a sharp increase in value. By 1946, the metal was quoted by the New York Exchange at a mean price of $.801 an ounce. This trend reflected the increasing demands of the silver users (i.e. industry and the U.S. Mint) as against world production. For a time, the Treasury tried to help out by selling silver from its own stockpile, but it soon became apparent that this practice could not continue indefinitely and, on November 28, 1961, it was discontinued.

As a result of Treasury curtailment, the price of silver rose sharply so that by 1964 it was $1.29 an ounce. Seeing the inevitability of further increases, and realizing that they would once again result in the melting down of coins, Congress now took the fateful step of introducing base-metal subsidiary issues. The action had of course the further advantage of saving hundreds of millions of ounces a year, which could thus be used for other purposes.

In 1967, the price of silver jumped to $1.55 (the annual average at the New York exchange), and further action was now deemed necessary. Of the total Treasury stockpile of about 520 million ounces, 430 million were then being held in reserve against the $555 million worth of outstanding silver certificates. On the assumption that most of these would never be presented for redemption, the Treasury Department asked Congress to order an end to the notes, permitting people to redeem them in bullion only for the length of one year. On June 24, 1967, Congress enacted legislation to this effect, and, with most of its $555 million in bullion reserve now released, the Treasury once again resumed its sale to the public.

As of mid-1968, the Treasury Department was well satisfied with its handling of the silver situation. It had stockpiled its objective of 165 million ounces of .999 silver, come up with the 17 million ounces required for the Kennedy half dollar coinage, and lost only 70 million ounces through the redemption of silver certificates.

However, by mid-1969, it was apparent that much of the silver sold by the Treasury, instead of going to the industries that most needed it, was actually being amassed by speculators. Missouri Representative Leonor Sullivan vigorously protested this "grievous blunder," as she saw it, but to no avail.

By March, 1970, the Treasury Department had already earmarked November 10 as a cut-off date for the sales. According to its calculations, the whole of its supply, except for the "fixed" national defense stockpile, would then be exhausted. However, when, during the same month, the Senate proposed striking 150,000,000 .400 fine Eisenhower dollars (which bill passed December 1970), the Treasury, on a revised upward estimate of the amount of silver recoverable from used photographic chemicals, agreed to release for the purpose 25.5. million ounces of .999 fine bullion from the stockpile.

Where does all this bring us to? The amount of silver required to mint 150 million Eisenhower dollars is 47,000,000 ounces. According to U.S. mint reports, the Treasury's program to recover silver from non-current coins in its possession began in earnest during the fiscal year 1968. In that year and the next it melted down some $226,000,000 worth of subsidiary coins which must have yielded about 170,000,000 ounces. At the same time, it still had on hand some 58,500,000 ounces with a promised 6,100,000 ounces yet in the Federal Reserves. All told, it should then have been able to stockpile over 226,000,000 ounces from its recovery program.

This, in fact, is the exact figure predicted by the Treasury Department as of March, 1969. However, by April 30, 1970, the estimate was reduced by some 13 million, a fact apparently overlooked in the last annual report. It was further calculated that at the close of the November sales, after due allowance for the 47,-400,000 ounces required for the Eisenhower dollars, there would be a reserve balance in the Treasury of 3,600,000 ounces.

All of which brings us to the recent fall of silver to the $1.314 level. Since I have predicted and will continue to predict an eventual sharp rise in the price of this metal, I can hardly leave the reader without some tentative explanation for this unusual event.

When, at the end of November, 1961, the Treasury Department suspended sales of silver bullion, it set the stage for an immediate escalation in the price of the metal. There is no inherent reason why the same result should not have followed the November, 1970 suspension, and less, certainly, for any prediction of an opposite trend. Yet, in mid-January, 1971, an anonymous American broker, parroting a prediction made the previous month by the head of the Silver Users Association, foresaw a possible drop in its value to $1.25 later in the year. Right afterwards, the price of silver did in fact tumble to a surprising $1.54 level.

Shall we believe that the same investors who ignored the earlier forecast were suddenly stampeded into widespread selling because of its reiteration by an unnamed source? This is wholly unlikely. The only alternative is that the anonymous prediction had no other connection with the drop except as a calculated ploy to justify it after it had been manipulated downward by the same source.

That such manipulations do take place is not only my own view but that also of the *Economic News Agency* which has been categoric on the point. In a speculative market where the vast majority of sales exist on paper alone, they are not, unfortunately, very difficult to perpetrate.

The only question remaining is who precisely is behind these tactics. The Dublin International Investment Councillors would indict the Government itself. According to these gentlemen, 65,-000,000 ounces of silver in our National Defense stockpile is actually contaminated from past use in atomic tests, leaving the Treasury Department with a critical shortage. Thus, the argument continues, the Government intends, at no distant date, to nationalize silver and is currently trying to push the price down to a point where, with the advent of N-day, it can rebuild its stockpile at a minimal cost. The nationalization is expected to come about after a flurry of short paper sales like those which produced the aforementioned drop to the $1.54 level. Whenever the price the administration was aiming for had been reached, all short positions would suddenly be ordered settled at the weekend's closing price.

What would this mean to those who had invested heavily in silver? Assuming as these gentlemen do that the price will first be knocked way down, it would naturally be a disaster. For though the action could hardly restrain a long-term rise in value, we would be prevented from trading freely in it except, perhaps, under the weight of an enormous tax.

If indeed, the Government were getting ready to nationalize silver, this is precisely the scenario we might expect. For my own part, however, I can only smile at the suggestion. In the first place, the rumor of the 65,000,000 ounces of contaminated silver has been going the rounds for several years now and it is quite unfounded. Even had the alleged contamination taken place, the silver would simply have been recycled to make it usable again. It should also be pointed out that most if not all of the silver returned to the Government by the Atomic Energy Commission has long ago been disposed of, and so has no relation to the current National Defense stockpile.

When we examine the argument in a broader context, it appears even more foolish. For it ignores the obvious fact that the Government has all along manifested a design to go out of the silver business, keeping only what it required for its stockpile and the projected coinage of Eisenhower dollars. Beyond this amount, it has retained a mere 3,000,000+ ounces, presumably to cover any small margin of error that might have crept into its calculations. Is it not highly illogical to imagine that it could either have been so deceived with respect to its own supply, or willingly placed itself in jeopardy? But even if this should be insisted upon, what is to stop the Government from doing precisely what every other silver user does and purchasing the amount it allegedly lacks? There is no dire shortage of silver on the commodity market, and no restrictions, certainly, against Uncle Sam.

But why in that case, the Dublin men ask, is the Treasury Department charging such exorbitant prices for the Eisenhower dollars? Is it not to discourage buyers and so curtail the coinage? This view could only be advanced by someone who is unfamiliar with American collectors. They will, no doubt, continue to complain against the prices, and justly so, but this will not prevent them from placing their orders. Nor is this fact overlooked by the powers that be. They know their customers and are simply going to make them pay through the nose.

With regard to manipulations then, the real culprits can only be among the silver users themselves who want above all to depress the price of the metal. This is not to say that the Government is necessarily unhappy about the decline. For let us not forget, when we speak of the vast consumption of silver by the photographic and electronics industries, that we mean in large measure a super-industry called the U.S. military establishment. I have not seen any exact figures on the silver usage by the Military and its contractors, but I suspect that the amount is a great deal larger than any of us would imagine.

Does this mean that at some remote period in our future silver might yet be nationalized? If by remote, we mean something like twenty-five years, then, of course, it is a possibility. In any case, we should have ample warning in the way of production-consumption statistics.

But even in the unlikely event that nationalization should come sooner (say in ten years!), should indeed be imposed without warning, it could have no adverse effect on one's investment in silver coins. For it seems to me wholly unlikely that any nationalization would be accompanied by the confiscation of silver coins. It is true that certain restrictions as to the possession of gold coins were announced by the Roosevelt administration when we went off the gold standard. But as silver is in no way connected with the balance of international payments, the situation is inherently different. Besides, even with respect to the gold coins, no real police action was ever undertaken to enforce the rule.

As already indicated, nationalization would have little effect on the long-term price of silver. The very fact that it could no longer be supplied by direct mining except at an excessive cost would force it upwards in the degree that total production lagged behind consumption. Eventually, it would have to reach a $5.00 price, or, perhaps, even the $10.00 an ounce predicted by the *Economic News Agency,* and that would be very nice for the holders of silver coins. Should a ban against melting again be ordered, the value of the coins could nevertheless be expected to keep pace with the value of silver.

If we will consult the tabular figures at the end of this chapter, we see that as of 1965, some $2,835,000,000 dollars worth of silver coins were still outstanding. Even if we subtract from this the figure of $283,000,000 which is apparently close to the actual value of the coins melted down during the silver recovery program, this would still leave a total of over $2½ billion worth of silver coins remaining. Of this amount, nearly a half billion represents silver dollars. Now it is exceedingly unlikely that any foreseeable rise in the price of silver could ever provoke the melting of the dollars because of their healthy numismatic premium plus the fact that this would also keep pace with any real escalation in the price of silver.

So we come to the remaining $2 billion worth of subsidiary coins. Although I can do no more than guess, I would expect that some $200,000,000 of this is locked up in numismatic collections and dealers' stocks of individual coins. The remainder, minus perhaps 25% which was illegally melted, must therefore consist of rolls and bags of coins. I don't know any good way of estimating how much is tied up respectively in each, but for argument's sake, let's split the figure in half. Since there is no real chance that the rolls will ever be melted down, we are left with a hypothetical figure of $625,000,000, which is still a few times larger than our National Defense stockpile.

Now let's suppose the price of silver has reached $3.00 an ounce, and the holders of these coins think it a good time to start melting them down. What would happen is that after a fairly short time, the sudden entry of all this silver would begin to depress the market and the melting would stop. After a time, when the price had gone back up, the melting would again start, and so on. However, in the case of nationalization, there would probably be something like a 50% tax on silver sales, and so melting would not begin until the price of silver reached an appreciably higher level.

We have seen how, despite the long-range prospects for silver, manipulation or a legitimate glutting from wholesale melting of coins can bring about temporary setbacks. With bags of silver coins, however, you are freed from such unpleasant effects. A bag of any denomination except the dollar contains $1,000. face value and weighs about 715 ozs. If the coins were uncirculated, they would weigh about 720 ozs., but as it is they all probably circulated somewhat. This needn't trouble us, however, since they are coins, not bullion, and can never lose their face value. But even if they did, your loss would be less than 6% (5% dealer's commission + .006% from attrition) plus the cost of melting. Or if you wanted to resell them as coins, it would cost you only 10%, the sum of two commissions. This is the worst that could happen, as against the best (which is much more likely), namely that by 1980 every bag for which you paid $1,000. would be worth $5,000. or more. Truly, this is the poor man's stock market, without, however, the attendant risks.

But there are some other and more immediate advantages that I must not neglect to mention. The average bag of silver coins will for the most part contain pieces in V.F.-E.F. condition. But the odds are that in among them will be a number of A.U. coins which are worth a premium in their own right. There will also be earlier issues, Mercury dimes and Standing Liberty half dollars which dealers are already beginning to differentiate as basically premium issues. Occasionally even earlier coins turn up, not to mention various rare dates and mintmarks. These are the bonus dividends, and they can be genuinely anticipated since the dealer who sells you the bag hasn't got time (for his 5%) to start looking himself. Remember that with silver coins no longer in circulation, these bags will be the prime source for finding scarce and rare items.

But suppose you can't afford an outlay of $1,000.00. In that case you can still buy a bag of silver nickels with $200. face value for $330.00. This might be a very good investment for a number of reasons. First, unlike the rest of the silver coins, silver nickels could always be legally melted, and large quantities have already suffered this fate. This is why it doesn't pay to purchase bags of regular nickels in the hope of finding a lot of silver ones. Secondly, as I have earlier pointed out, they comprise an interesting and unique type set. Finally, the value of this set is currently depressed, and selling for only 50% of its 1964 peak price.

A word remains to be said regarding bags of silver dollars. These are currently available at $3,000., and numismatically may represent the best of such investments. Which reminds me of a story I think you will find interesting.

Back in March, 1964, I learned "through channels," as they say, that there were only about $2,000,000 worth of Peace dollars left among the coins being distributed by the Treasury. Naturally, I was very anxious for this amount to be sold so that the Morgans would start appearing. But two million dollars is a lot of money, more, in any case, than I had to spend. So I approached the head of a prominent New York silver mining company and proposed that if they would lay out the amount, thereby getting the Peace dollars out of the way, a very profitable joint venture might be formed out of what would follow.

In letting him in on the secret, I of course took a calculated risk, for there was nothing to prevent him, once he had the knowledge, from undercutting me entirely. The third alternative, namely that he would do nothing, was the least expected, but such, curiously turned out to be the case.

But, as fate would have it, a prominent investment sheet just about this time made reference to me as a well-known dealer in bags of silver dollars. As a result, I suddenly received an unprecedented number of orders for these bags. Well, before too long, the Peace dollars were exhausted, and sure enough there followed the Morgans. In fact, not *only* Morgans but seated Libertys as well! And lest the reader think I took too great advantage of the situation, let me state that I continued to sell my bags of dollars *mint-sealed,* and many are the collectors who can testify that for their $1,050. they received not only the earlier coins, but even such rare dates as 1893-S and 1871-CC! The end of the story, however, is not an undilutedly happy one. For a certain Philadelphia dealer, having gotten wind of the situation, proceeded to call every other dealer he could think of in order to sell the bags. Naturally, these men were not stupid, and when they began to compare notes they quickly realized the situation. So the rush was on, and before too long the bonanza was exhausted. Nowadays the Mint has become more canny, as we may observe from its current plan to auction off its remaining 3,000,000 rare-date Carson City dollars.

SILVER STATISTICS, 1921-1969

Year (Fiscal)	Silver $1 in Circulation	Silver $1 Minted	Silver $1 Melted	Silver Subsidiary Coins in Circ.	Silver Subsidiary Coins Minted	Silver Subsidiary Coins Melted (Incl. Trade $1)	Aver. Value of 1 oz. Silver at N.Y. Exchange (Calendar Year)
1921	$288,788,378	$19,043,000		$271,314,375	$13,389,070	$634,168	$.631
1922	381,174,404	92,388,473	$2,447	271,210,886	160,093	2,568,978	.679
1923	491,886,769	110,715,000	2,635	269,186,084	675,000	3,505,710	.652
1924	503,754,851	11,870,000	1,918	277,614,378	10,276,040	2,222,192	.671
1925	522,061,078	18,308,000	1,773	283,471,971	8,221,404	2,648,953	.694
1926	533,491,184	11,432,700	2,594	288,923,000	7,750,478	2,744,136	.624
1927	537,944,446	4,456,900	3,638	295,589,859	9,572,659	3,933,231	.567
1928	539,961,701	2,018,649	1,394	299,010,231	6,937,418	4,223,116	.585
1929	539,960,849	—	852	304,187,449	7,488,700	3,802,167	.533
1930	539,959,520	—	1,329	310,978,375	9,177,500	4,346,366	.385
1931	539,958,327	—	1,193	308,619,365	795,300	5,486,303	.290
1932	540,007,911	—	442	304,882,996	803,000	7,481,995	.282
1933	540,007,398	—	513	298,634,122	1,158,200	8,466,932	.350
1934	540,006,894	—	504	294,770,252	3,136,925	7,563,233	.483
1935	545,651,802	5,635,557	649	312,416,169	26,273,810	8,827,565	.646
1936	547,080,164	1,439,000	638	331,716,093	26,152,805	7,199,556	.454
1937	547,079,825	—	339	358,899,286	32,962,267	6,026,548	.452
1938	547,079,218	—	607	373,461,485	19,854,941	5,514,079	.435
1939	547,078,589	—	629	379,811,988	11,029,058	4,861,144	.394
1940	547,078,223	—	366	402,261,461	26,807,671	4,530,604	.351
1941	547,077,816	—	407	447,247,860	49,211,552	4,122,532	.351
1942	547,077,254	—	562	529,814,276	85,307,259	2,767,266	.386
1943	538,996,271	—	8,080,983	659,967,847	133,341,140	2,538,594	.451

Year							
1944	494,337,395	—	734,488,137	44,658,876	77,596,800	1,704,574	.451
1945	493,943,078	—	825,798,486	394,317	97,380,400	1,968,970	.519
1946	493,580,063	—	878,958,125	97,072	55,305,150	1,778,730	.801
1947	493,462,387	—	922,656,000	68,589	52,736,148	1,830,988	.718
1948	493,100,146	—	952,298,876	362,240	30,727,333	2,771,416	.744
1949	492,857,480	—	989,455,582	242,666	38,984,513	2,111,643	.719
1950	492,582,858	—	1,001,573,600	274,623	14,902,117	2,771,444	.742
1951	492,248,551	—	1,041,945,901	334,439	42,792,412	2,347,425	.895
1952	491,896,851	—	1,117,889,100	351,642	77,942,796	1,810,775	.850
1953	491,517,862	—	1,193,757,500	378,993	77,581,610	1,292,034	.853
1954	491,020,651	—	1,275,666,000	498,034	83,689,857	1,304,959	.853
1955	490,347,400	—	1,296,140,300	669,317	23,275,900	1,667,716	.891
1956	488,650,400	—	1,317,444,900	24,165,093	11,403,124	53,463,574	.908
1957	488,435,800	—	1,382,455,600	216,481	18,885,135	10,540,279	.908
1958	488,246,700	—	1,448,812,500	190,531	68,270,119	1,702,356	.890
1959	488,046,100	—	1,496,953,100	322,669	50,499,572	2,074,554	.912
1960	487,773,300	—	1,552,105,600	191,585	56,637,536	1,378,264	.914
1961	487,589,300	—	1,608,670,200	196,520	58,456,146	1,481,704	.924
1962	487,355,300	—	1,710,760,400	333,175	103,916,104	1,704,118	1.085
1963	486,017,400	—	1,824,877,900	1,080,724	115,701,405	1,452,062	1.279
1964	484,722,100	—	1,999,475,000	1,293,378	198,966,287	1,002,180	1.293
1965	—	—	2,350,338,879	—	354,895,290	506,553	1.293
1966	—	—	—	—	—	390,159	1.293
1967	—	—	—	—	—	517,315	1.550
1968	—	—	—	—	—	43,135,649	2.145
1969	—	—	—	—	—	182,800,000	1.790

NOTE: Theoretically, the figures for coins in circulation should equal the sum of the previous and present year minus the melt figure. However, discrepancies exist, especially for the subsidiary coins, and it is evident that additional calculations included certain exports and imports, general disappearance, and perhaps revised estimates based on coins in the Federal Reserve.

Chapter 2
How to Learn Right

Wayte Raymond, one of the canniest dealers of his generation, used often to remark that the best investment in numismatics was knowledge. Today, when so many in-depth studies have been made of the different series of U.S. coins, as well as many branches of foreign and ancient numismatics, his saying is truer than ever. With knowledge you can buy right, sell right, collect right and be miles ahead of the collector or dealer who contents himself with a one or two book library.

Through the years, I've found that most collectors not only do not try to educate themselves numismatically, but are not even aware of the possibilities that exist for such an education. For those of you who fall into this category, I would suggest as a starting point, a simple trip to the library of the American Numismatic Society in New York. The reason is that the A.N.S. library is actually larger than many branch libraries you will find in your own city—even if its a large one. Just to see the thousands of volumes that are available on the many different phases of the subject is an education as it wakens us to how little we really know, and how much more our studious fellow collectors may already have learned.

What does it matter how much the next fellow knows? In a competitive field like numismatics, it matters considerably. The people who will be selling you coins are looking for the best deal they can get. You can hardly expect them to educate you, to tell you, say,

Year							
1944	494,337,395	—	44,658,876	734,488,137	77,596,800	1,704,574	.451
1945	493,943,078	—	394,317	825,798,486	97,380,400	1,968,970	.519
1946	493,580,063	—	97,072	878,958,125	55,305,150	1,778,730	.801
1947	493,462,387	—	68,589	922,656,000	52,736,148	1,830,988	.718
1948	493,100,146	—	362,240	952,298,876	30,727,333	2,771,416	.744
1949	492,857,480	—	242,666	989,455,582	38,984,513	2,111,643	.719
1950	492,582,858	—	274,623	1,001,573,600	14,902,117	2,771,444	.742
1951	492,248,551	—	334,439	1,041,945,901	42,792,412	2,347,425	.895
1952	491,896,851	—	351,642	1,117,889,100	77,942,796	1,810,775	.850
1953	491,517,862	—	378,993	1,193,757,500	77,581,610	1,292,034	.853
1954	491,020,651	—	498,034	1,275,666,000	83,689,857	1,304,959	.853
1955	490,347,400	—	669,317	1,296,140,300	23,275,900	1,667,716	.891
1956	488,650,400	—	24,165,093	1,317,444,900	11,403,124	53,463,574	.908
1957	488,435,800	—	216,481	1,382,455,600	18,885,135	10,540,279	.908
1958	488,246,700	—	190,531	1,448,812,500	68,270,119	1,702,356	.890
1959	488,046,100	—	322,669	1,496,953,100	50,499,572	2,074,554	.912
1960	487,773,300	—	191,585	1,552,105,600	56,637,536	1,378,264	.914
1961	487,589,300	—	196,520	1,608,670,200	58,456,146	1,481,704	.924
1962	487,355,300	—	333,175	1,710,760,400	103,916,104	1,704,118	1.085
1963	486,017,400	—	1,080,724	1,824,877,900	115,701,405	1,452,062	1.279
1964	484,722,100	—	1,293,378	1,999,475,000	198,966,287	1,002,180	1.293
1965	—	—	—	2,350,338,879	354,895,290	506,553	1.293
1966	—	—	—	—	—	390,159	1.293
1967	—	—	—	—	—	517,315	1.550
1968	—	—	—	—	—	43,135,649	2.145
1969	—	—	—	—	—	182,800,000	1.790

NOTE: Theoretically, the figures for coins in circulation should equal the sum of the previous and present year minus the melt figure. However, discrepancies exist, especially for the subsidiary coins, and it is evident that additional calculations included certain exports and imports, general disappearance, and perhaps revised estimates based on coins in the Federal Reserve.

Chapter 2
How to Learn Right

Wayte Raymond, one of the canniest dealers of his generation, used often to remark that the best investment in numismatics was knowledge. Today, when so many in-depth studies have been made of the different series of U.S. coins, as well as many branches of foreign and ancient numismatics, his saying is truer than ever. With knowledge you can buy right, sell right, collect right and be miles ahead of the collector or dealer who contents himself with a one or two book library.

Through the years, I've found that most collectors not only do not try to educate themselves numismatically, but are not even aware of the possibilities that exist for such an education. For those of you who fall into this category, I would suggest as a starting point, a simple trip to the library of the American Numismatic Society in New York. The reason is that the A.N.S. library is actually larger than many branch libraries you will find in your own city—even if its a large one. Just to see the thousands of volumes that are available on the many different phases of the subject is an education as it wakens us to how little we really know, and how much more our studious fellow collectors may already have learned.

What does it matter how much the next fellow knows? In a competitive field like numismatics, it matters considerably. The people who will be selling you coins are looking for the best deal they can get. You can hardly expect them to educate you, to tell you, say, that an item for which they want $200. might be obtained from various other sources for half that price. It is up to you to know the true value of a coin you wish to buy, to know whether or not it is correctly attributed and fairly graded, to know whether it or some other piece would be more appropriate to your collection.

The same holds in selling. Let's say you value your collection at X dollars, but the person to whom you offer it comes up with a much lower figure. How do you know whether your valuations are inflated or whether his are on the conservative side? How will you know whether your collection would do best in a public auction, sold outright, or left with a dealer on a consignment basis?

There is only one way, and that is through education. As a starting point, you will need Richard Yeoman's *A Guide Book to United States Coins,* which is easily the best popular work on U.S. numismatics. When you've absorbed all it has to offer and are beginning to feel confident in your knowledge, then its time to move on to a graduate course. For this you will require the new *Scott's Comprehensive Catalogue and Encyclopedia of U.S. Coins* by Don Taxay, and you will be doing quite well if you finish it in a year's time. Even in areas like colonial coins and early U.S. mint issues, where the work makes no pretense of listing every die variety, it offers a great deal of important data that is not found in the specialized "standard works." Moreover, its sections on essays (i.e. patterns, trials and experimental pieces) and private American gold issues are books in themselves, supplanting everything previously written on the subject. Literally hundreds of coins are listed which are to be found in no other current catalogue. Another valuable feature of this book is that it notes wherever a particular issue becomes very rare or unobtainable above a given condition. Other catalogues are in the habit of listing most items in every condition, even in cases where they might not exist in the highest grades. The result is that many collectors by-pass what may be the finest available specimen of a coin in the vain hope of sometime finding an uncirculated one.

But as valuable as even this book is, it will still be to your advantage to buy certain specialized works on die varieties—Sheldon and Newcomb on large cents, Gilbert and Bowers on half cents, Browning on quarters, Overton on half dollars, Bolender on dollars, Breen on the gold denominations.

If you collect colonial coins, you will need the works of Crosby, Noe, Newman, Maris, Miller and Ryder, to name but the most important. And you will want to keep up to date by subscribing to the *Colonial Newsletter.* If tokens interest you, read the works of Hetrich-Guttag and Fuld and subscribe to the journal of the Token and Medal Society.

"But," you may argue, "I don't collect die varietes, so why should I have specialized works?" The reason is that the rarity between die varieties differs enormously, and by learning these differences you will be able to buy many rare items which have not been fully attributed and are priced like common ones. Astute collectors and dealers call this "cherry picking," and it will enable you too, by judicious buying and selling, to build up a valuable collection at a minimum cost.

You will also have to learn the fine art of accurately grading the condition of coins. Probably no abuse is so rampant in the field as overgrading, and where the price variation between two grades is 100%, it is obviously essential that you can recognize the difference.

Over the past century, continuous overgrading has caused what might be called a debasement of the terminology. For example, a coin that used to be graded "good" a century ago would today be called "fine", perhaps even "very fine." It seems to me that there are five common reasons why coins continue to be overgraded, and why buyer and seller so often disagree on the subject. They are: 1. The seller has never learned to grade properly. 2. He thinks you've never learned to do so. 3. He's near-sighted. 4. He thinks you're nearsighted. 5. He honestly has different standards than you do on the subject. An excellent book, which has been recently published on grading, is *Photograde* by James Ruddy. The enlarged photographs are very useful and every collector should obtain a copy of the work.

However, even knowing what detail should appear on a coin in a given grade is not enough. The reason is that many dates are poorly struck up at the Mint, and are not perfectly sharp even in uncirculated condition. Scott's *Comprehensive Catalogue* is very useful in this respect, as it notes wherever this occurs frequently among the various Mint issues. But the striking quality of a coin is only one of the factors, independent of wear, that can influence the grade, and hence the value of a coin. Another is lint marks caused by tiny threads sticking to the die after it has been wiped with a cloth. This is a fairly common defect among Indian head cents, and it is good to be able to recognize it.

Again, many of the very early Mint issues are frequently marred by "adjustment marks," i.e. parallel lines caused by filing the planchet (at the Mint) to bring it down to its proper weight. Adjustment marks can be recognized as distinct from later scratches, file marks etc., since, unlike the latter, they do not become deeper in the areas of relief.

More common than either lint marks or adjustment marks are bag marks, which take in all the little nicks suffered by a coin before it leaves the Mint. These are particularly noticeable on the larger silver and gold coins, i.e. the silver dollars, eagles and double eagles. In fact, it is sometimes very difficult to obtain a specimen of a given year with a really attractive surface appearance even though you may chose entirely from among uncirculated coins.

Thus we see that wear is not the only thing that determines the condition of a coin—and thus its value. The best attributors always consider these other factors, and will sometimes distinguish between no less than four different grades of uncirculated, viz. "so-so," "choice," "gem," and "superb." At public auctions, especially, a superb unc. is quite liable to realize twice the amount brought by an ordinary so-so specimen.

The novice collector would do well to examine the surface of a good many coins of the type (and date) he is interested in collecting before making an investment. In this way, he will familiarize himself with the average surface characteristics, and be able to immediately recognize superior and inferior specimens of a given grade.

Though "proof" is not really a condition, but a special surface finishing and method of striking, it is, unfortunately, quite often treated as the former. And just as many extremely fine coins are offered for sale as uncirculated, so many uncirculated pieces are pawned off as proofs. This is really a serious matter, and it always make me wonder why more collectors do not spend a little time in learning to recognize the characteristics of a genuine proof coin. For one thing, a proof not only has a special surface (highly polished, matte or sandblast), but has been struck several blows on a hydraulic press resulting in bolder detail and a wire rim. If you lay it next to a regular coin, you will see that it is broader at the edge. First strikes may have a mirror finish, but they will lack the boldness and wire rim of a proof.

Now let's talk about cleaned coins. Judging from my own experience with collectors, I would say that more than half today cannot tell, as a rule, when a piece has been cleaned. The reason is probably that by now the *majority* of the older coins in numismatic circulation have in fact been cleaned, some more than once, so that the possibility of comparing cleaned to uncleaned coins is growing progressively more difficult.

And yet, we are told as almost the first rule of collecting never to clean a coin! Obviously when theory and practice clash so dramatically something further needs to be said on the subject. Let me start by saying that it is not the cleaning of a coin which is harmful, but the effect of cleaning it the wrong way. Moreover, as gold, silver and copper (or bronze) all have different properties, what may be successful on one will damage another.

Gold coins, for example, can never really tarnish to any extent, and what little discoloration occurs can easily be removed by a bath in ammonia or dilute acid. Uncirculated silver coins, if merely tarnished, can benefit from the same operation. Less desirable are the "dips" which actually coat the surface with a thin micro-layer of silver, and still less any method of actually rubbing the surface with an abrasive. In both instances, the coin will soon begin to tarnish all over again, and in the latter case it will show ugly streaks or hairlines. If a coin is heavily incrusted, the safest method of cleaning is by an electrolytic bath. This will not necessarily restore the coin to pristine condition (for what has been eaten away by corrosion is gone forever), but whatever can be saved will be.

Copper and bronze coins tarnish the fastest and are the hardest to clean successfully. Never use acids, even when the coin is in mint condition. A little oil, applied with a soft cloth, will remove light dirt, and a toothpick can be used for the more stubborn residue. There is also a very good patented product called "Care" which, when used in this way, coats the coin with a permanent layer of oil and silica. Some persons prefer not to use it on brilliant coins, as it tends to darken them slightly, but if you do not mind this there can be no more serious objection. Corrosion, of course, is not likely to yield to anything less than electrolysis, without damaging the coin in the process. The new collector should make an effort to acquaint himself with all these techniques. Whether or not he actually uses them, his familiarity will enable him to detect their use on the various coins he is offered. Remember, all bright coins are not uncirculated, and if you can't tell the difference, watch out! When offered an allegedly mint state coin, look first of all at all the high points to make sure the relief is intact. But bear in mind that many coins are weakly struck, and even when new will appear no more sharp than other extremely fine specimens. In such a case, your only criterion will be surface quality.

Years ago, my good friend Don Taxay showed me the best way to determine when in fact a softly struck coin is actually uncirculated. You hold the coin at a slight angle, so that it catches the light, and then rotate it very slowly. If it is truly uncirculated, the tiny radial "rivers" on the surface caused by the metal flow during striking will produce a "cartwheel" effect. But if the coin is even slightly worn, these lines will be broken and light will not be reflected in this way. Try it and see. Eventually you'll be able to tell very quickly whether a coin is truly uncirculated, even when it is highly tarnished. On the other hand, a slightly worn coin, no matter how cleverly cleaned, will never again deceive you. Make a real effort to learn to grade properly. Nothing is more important if you are going to make that investment of yours really grow.

Finally, you will have to learn how to spot a counterfeit or altered coin. These are, unfortunately, becoming more and more common, not to mention deceptive. Since Mr. Taxay has written a comprehensive book on the subject (*Counterfeit, Mis-struck and Unofficial U.S. Coins,* 1963), it will be enough to point out here that, ultimately, the only way to recognize a fake is by knowing the characteristics of the genuine. Once again, education plus practical experience is the keynote.

As my old friend and one of the ablest numismatic book dealers, Aaron Feldman, likes to say, "Buy the book before the coin." Not many collectors have yet learned this valuable piece of advice, but a few, taking quite literally this dictum, have shortly blossomed out into very able numismatists. Such persons become "seasoned" almost from the start, and when any opportunity arises, they are always ready to take advantage of it.

Chapter 3
How to Profit with
Rolls of Uncirculated Coins

When we speak of uncirculated rolls, we mean, with few exceptions, relatively recent issues. Roll collecting represents an intermediate ground between the hoarding of bags of coins and serious numismatics. It leans towards the former in the sense that the profit motive predominates, and towards the latter in that the coins are considered with respect to date, mint, and, of course, condition.

The performance of rolls must necessarily differ somewhat from that of most numismatic items. For one thing, persons who purchase rolls do not attempt to obtain the same quantity of each issue within a series. Instead, they concentrate on those items which they feel are most likely to show a quick and substantial profit, changing from one to another as the circumstances suggest. This is why the various issues tend to move not only as a group, but also relatively to one another.

The knowledgeable investor may thus be expected to unload all or part of a particular issue as soon as its value tends to level off, reinvesting his capital in others that seem more promising at the moment. However, when too much money has gone into certain issues and a good deal of it is suddenly pulled out, this tends to cause their decline at the same time that the formerly neglected issues begin to rise. To what extent the old favorites will fall depends on how much of the capital invested in them is withdrawn, and this in turn is a matter not only of reallocation, but also of how much new capital is entering the series or old capital departing from it. In other words, the more dollars you have chasing the same goods, the greater their tendency towards inflation, and vice versa.

What is it that causes these levelling off periods in the first place? Why, when a coin is hot and is constantly increasing in value, should new money not continue to be invested in it indefinitely? The reason is "Forman's law of limitations," which states that when any particular issue gets too far ahead of the rest, it tends to make the latter appear underpriced by comparison. As a result, investors begin to turn their eyes to the depressed issues. The way-in-front coins cease to find their formerly bullish market and consequently will no longer continue to rise. Then, with the levelling off, a good many investors may begin to unload which, as I have said, tends to actually reverse the momentum of the issues for a time. The intelligent investor will thus keep a close eye on market activity and not be lulled by those "counsellors" who talk about a perennial "profit march" of coins, as though the profits for each individual issue were guaranteed by some imaginery super-savings bank.

Since Lincoln cents comprise the single most popular series of U.S. coins, we may appropriately begin our analysis with them. By consulting our tables of annual price averages, we can see that it was not until the late 1950's that roll collecting was taken up in earnest. Before that time, rolls were purchased, as a rule, only by dealers who would then break them up and sell the coins individually to collectors. Between 1940 and 1950, the collective value of uncirculated rolls of cents from 1934 to 1940 (the most readily available) merely doubled, or showed an annual increase of 10%. (Even then, however, their return was far better than that offered by any savings bank.) Moreover, there seems to have been little appreciation of the scarcer issues, apparently because the number of collectors was still too few to make any real difference. Thus we find such low-mintage cents as the 1938-D and S and 1939-D actually selling for less than the much commoner 1937 coin. By 1950 this situation had been largely corrected and, despite the still depressed state of the market, a truer appreciation of relative rarities is apparent.

We jump next to 1954, this year being not so much important

in itself as for comparison to the following. For example, the 1954 price total shows a 48% increase over that of 1950, or 12% per year. This is only 2% higher than the yearly average of the 1940's, and based on it no one could have guessed what a fantastic boom was in the making. However, it is interesting to note that four different dates, 1934-D, '35-D, '35-S and 38-D, were being carefully garnered away by dealers so that they have no sales records for the period. (Whenever this occurs I have inserted NA=No Activity into the tabular listing.) It is clear that all of these low-mintage items were thought to be much underpriced, and were being hoarded in anticipation of a substantial increase in their value. As it finally turned out, the 1935-D and 1938-D were less rare in mint state than their mintages would suggest, a fact which emerged from the closer scrutiny made possible by the increasing volume of roll transactions. What strikes me as really strange, however, is that no one at this comparatively late date had noticed the 1939-D which is every bit as rare as its 15.2 million mintage would indicate.

The year 1955 heralded the start of the great roll boom, and this seems to have been the direct result of the unusually low mintages for the year. Not only were all these issues quickly snatched up by the initiated, but attention in general was focussed on the roll market. From December 1954 to December 1955 we find an overall increase in the cent roll market of some 73%. Compare this to the annual increases of the earlier years and you will begin to understand the sudden enormous interest in rolls generated at this time.

Another basis for comparison is the number of roll dealers active, respectively, at the end of 1954 and at the peak of the boom. Browsing through the December, 1954 issue of *Numismatic Scrapbook Magazine,* I find no more than a half dozen dealers featuring rolls, namely Max Hirschhorn and S.H. Feinberg (the early deans of the roll dealers), J.S. Schirmer, C.N. Thorsen, R.J. Salisbury and the Crystal Coin Co. By 1964, this select group had blossomed into such a huge fraternity that it is difficult to recall all of its members. In addition to myself, however, I must mention Alan J. Rosenberg, Hy London, Ralph Graf, Harry Warner, Victor Sandlin, Richard Duszynski, Ray Kotansky, Joe Gaidar, Blaise J. Dantone, L. Friedman, Ken Dolbee, Joe Flynn Sr., Jules Steinman, George Justus, Jonah R. Shapiro, Tommy Ryan, the late Michael Kolman and the late James F. Kelly. These are only a few of the names that immediately occur to me; a more comprehensive list would doubtless include almost every dealer who was then active in the numismatic field.

By the end of 1956, the cent rolls had again increased some 25%, which is not bad for a year of consolidation. This was followed, in 1957, by a new gain of no less than 90%. The largest profit-taking was by the pre-1940 coins, where an actual shortage of rolls (as apart from their mere hoarding) caused increases in every case of over 100%. Once again, a year of consolidation followed, 1958 netting an increase of only about 24%. The year 1959 showed a new gain of 44½% at which point the cent rolls seemed to have gone about as far as they could. For the next two years no new money entered the series which, as a whole, remained perfectly quiet. Despite this immobility, however, a sharp reallocation of capital was taking place in the direction of the scarcer early issues, specifically the 1934 and 1935 cents (which disappeared from the market) and the 1938-S, 1939-D and 1942-S.

After a dormant two years, the cent rolls once again came alive. In 1962, the series netted a 36% increase, while 1963 chalked up a fantastic 149%, representing not only the largest single-year increase but an all-time high for the cent rolls. In a sense you might say that 1963 was too good, at least for the earlier dates, which were pushed up all out of proportion to the rest of the series. Thus, in accordance with Forman's law of limitations, investors transferred their capital to the neglected issues (including most of the quarters and half dollars) causing a decline in the early date cents.

If the roll market as a whole (i.e. all five denominations) showed an increase of 22% in 1964, it was, nevertheless the beginning of the end. And just as forecasters in 1954 could hardly have anticipated the boom to come, so too, in early 1964, it would have been difficult to imagine anything short of a national catastrophe that could have reversed the upward trend of uncirculated rolls.

What happened is that the Treasury Department singled out roll investors as the prime suspects in the continuing coin shortage, and induced Congress to pass remedial legislation to discourage them. The plan, which temporarily abolished mintmarks, succeeded even better than was hoped (by the Mint that is). Investors, anticipating a predictable loss of interest in the field, started to unload, and when enough of them had done so it brought about the very decline they themselves had feared.

Then, in 1968, a strange thing happened. As a result of the general disinterest in rolls, few people had continued to put away large quantities of the new coins until, inevitably, it was discovered that these neglected issues had actually become scarce! On a lesser scale, it was 1955 all over again. The year 1968 brought new blood and better prices for the whole field. Presumably this trend would have continued right up to the present were it not for the recession which developed the following year and has been with us ever since.

When we turn to the nickels and dimes, the story is essentially the same as for the cents, i.e. a steep climb from 1955 to 1963, a decline in much of the higher priced material in 1964, and then a general falling off. On the other hand, virtually all of the quarters and half dollars advanced during 1964 so that these two series really monopolized profit-taking. Once again, the reason must be sought in the law of limitations. In other words, the quarters and halves, which had been relatively overlooked due to their high face value, now seemed very attractive to the smart money and were pushed up in part by the same capital that had departed from the cents and dimes. That even after 1964 half dollar rolls were still considered worth holding is evident from their comparatively small decline from 1964 to 1970. Compare the statistics for this denomination with that of any other and you will be surprised by its performance.

Now let us talk about strategy which, as a would-be roll investor, you will find indispensable. We have already seen that the roll market differs considerably from that of most numismatic fields because of the constant changes that are taking place in the relative values of the different issues and series'. This means that every investor is in a sense in competition to be the first either in buying or selling. If a roll has good profit potential, the investor who buys earliest makes the greatest profit. Again, if it is ready to decline, it pays to be an early seller. In this light, the smart investor emerges as the maker of trends rather than as their follower.

But even if you have been napping while a certain issue has begun to move, the game may be far from lost. Those who tell you, as a rule of thumb, only to do your buying when the majority are selling, and vice versa, are giving some very uncritical advice. Isn't it smarter to buy a hot item even when it has used up half its steam than, at that point, to start selling it?

Our first job is thus to determine which items are currently undervalued in relation to the rest. To the layman it might seem that this requires nothing more than a comparison of the various mintage figures. However, if one builds such a simple ratio system in his mind, and uses it as the basis for his investment, he will doubtless go astray. This is due to the fact that the correspondence between the quantity of an issue originally struck and that still surviving in mint state is often variable. For example, the farther back we go, the fewer the coins we must expect to have been salted away. Moreover, within the same year, uncirculated coins will always be rarer within the higher denominations.

The systematic hoarding of new issues seems to have begun in the early 1950's, and, after 1955, to have reached epidemic proportions. Thus, from this time until 1965, when roll collecting sharply fell off, mintages do not really tell us very much. Even beyond these circumstances, and for a variety of reasons, certain issues just seem to be rarer or commoner than their mintages would suggest. For instance, even in the early days, a notoriously low mintage might induce the hoarding of a coin out of all proportion to one with a huge population. This occurred in the case of the rare 1931-S cent (a depression issue to boot), which is still available in uncirculated rolls.

From all of this, the reader might infer that mintage figures may be quite ignored as a factor of value. This, however, would be as incorrect as an insistence on using them in a hard and fast way. Mintage figures are indeed a factor to be reckoned with; they are simply not the only one.

In that case, you might think, the best approach would be in comparing the various ratios for each of the earlier years. This, as I long ago learned, is an interesting experiment, but one which leads ultimately to confusion. The reason is that even if we add up all the numerous totals and draw mean figures, our calculations will have been distorted by the lack of discrimination so evident in the early years.

How then is one to really determine the investment potential of the various issues? There is a way and I will now disclose it. If you examine the annual returns at the end of this chapter, you will see that the peak years for virtually all the issues are 1963-64. However, between the reports of these two years, there is, for our purposes at least, a world of difference. In 1963, various of the scarcer cents, nickels and dimes were being driven upwards out of all proportion to their merits. This situation, as already noted, was largely corrected during the next twelve months when, according to the law of limitations, justice was done to the neglected issues. Moreover, by the end of 1964, enthusiasm for rolls had already begun to waver in the face of the Treasury Department's threat to destroy the identifying features of the different issues. All-in-all then, the year was one of prudence and reckoning, and may be admitted, with few exceptions, as the most accurate single reading of relative rarities. This I am able to confirm by my long acquaintance with the market and knowledge of the comparative availability and existence of various issues.

Now let us turn to our predictions. Among the cents, we observe a group of earlier dates which have uniformly fallen about 70% from 1964 to 1970 and which, by comparison to their more common contemporaries, seem underpriced. Specifically, I mean the 1936-S, '37-S and '38-D and S.

But there are some later dates which are even more worthy of our consideration. For example, look at the 1946-S. Having been underpriced from the start, and then dropping no less than 83% from 1964, this roll is now selling at a mere $3.25*. This is only a fraction of that of many issues which are considerably more common. Moral: this is a blue-chip item if there ever was one. Another issue which is in the same class is the 1954-S. It has dropped an amazing 84%, falling from $22.00 in 1964 to the present $3.50! Coming now to the nickels, I would first of all recommend the 1938-D and S, which have been grossly underpriced ever since anyone can remember. Take a look at their mintages, only 5.4 and 4.1 million respectively, and a very good reflection of their rarity. Is there any inherent reason why these pieces should not be in the

---

* By "now," I mean August 1971, at which time this book went to press.

same price class as the 1939-S? But such are the fortunes of speculation that the latter alone has received all the attention. Eventually,
however, this situation cannot but correct itself.

My next nickel choices are the 1946-S, '47-S, '48-S and '49-S,
all of which have declined far more than they deserve. The 1946-S
has dropped some 69%, and is selling at the present time for only
$24.50 a roll. Take a look at its 13.6 million mintage and tell me
if that's not a bargain price, especially as it is hardly any more
than for the comparatively common 1945-S. The 1947-S is admit-
tedly somewhat less rare, but still ought to be worth somewhat
more than its current asking price. Note that this item dropped
no less than 83% from 1964. The 1948-S is what I call a real
sleeper. Just 11.3 million struck, and yet its 1971 price is only
$23.00 compared to $30.00 for the common '48-D! So please don't
pass these up;—they are bound to take off! Finally, we have the
1949-S with its miniscule mintage of 9.7 million. This issue has
dropped 74% from 1964, and, in my eyes, is underpriced at
$42.50. When we consider that the average pre-1955 nickel lost
little more than 50%, the implications of the above will be obvious.

The 1950-P nickel is in the same class as the 1949-S. It has an
almost identical mintage, and currently sells for the same price.
Need I add, "same comment as for the previous?"

I don't know that I wouldn't also call the 1951-S underpriced.
This item is even scarcer than its 7.8 mintage would indicate, and
is nothing to walk away from even though it sells for quite a bit more
than the previous two. Shouldn't the fact that it dropped 81½%
since 1964 tell us something about its predictable future?

But a still better buy is the 1955-P, which has an almost identical mintage. This issue has dropped 80% since 1964 and looks like
a very good investment from where I sit.

Now we come to the dimes. As a rule of thumb, any Roosevelt
dime which has lost two thirds or more of its 1964 value should at
the very least be worthy of our consideration. The first coin I would
recommend is the 1946-D, which would seem to have everything
working in its favor. Not only does it show a drop of 67%, but
this as against a gain, from 1955 to 1964, of only four times, or
about two thirds the average. A good indication of its solid worth
is the fact that it doubled in value from 1963 to 1964, the record

for a Roosevelt dime during this year of reckoning. Finally, its 1971 value reads only about a third higher than that for 1955.

I would also rate the 1946-S, which shows a net loss of 76% from 1964. This is certainly a far better buy than the '47-D which is currently selling for about 50% more.

Next is the 1947-P. True, it has a 121.5 million mintage, but remember it is not a first-year type coin, and relatively few people were putting away rolls in those days. I believe that the main reason why this item has suffered is due to its too bullish climb in 1963. However, after dropping 60% in one year, it hardly deserves to have fallen another 74% since then. Evidently this item has been pegged as a loser, but loser or no, there is no conceivable reason why it should be selling today for 20% less than its 1955 price!

1947-S is a real sleeper. First of all, its mintage is only 34.8 million, a modest enough figure for a Roosevelt time. Secondly, after rising only 3.2 times from 1955 to 1964, it has suffered a 72% loss from that year to the present.

Of the big three, 1949-S, '50-S and '51-S, the first seem to have held its ground comparatively well since 1964 while the last two have slipped badly. The 1950-S lost 66⅔%, the '51-S 74½%. Both items look like good bets to me. The 1952-S, with its 63% drop and the 1953-S with 66% should also be watched.

1954-S and 1955 P-D-S are all scheduled for a good sharp rise, and you have only to look at their prices to see why. Since 1964 these four items lost, respectively, 65%, 76%, 76% and 74%. All are therefore very good items, the '55-D perhaps the best.

The first of the Washington quarter that looks a little under-priced is the 1940-S. This coin is a bit rarer than both the '41-S and D, but for some strange reason has dropped well below the latter. Also underpriced are the '44-S, '47-S, 1954-S and 1955, all of which have fallen too much since their 1964 peak. However, I am inclined to think that the biggest sleeper in the whole series is the 1958-P. While virtually every other post-1955 quarter has more or less held its own, the '58-P managed to lose 53%. So watch this one. It can only go up!

Compare the 1948 and '48-D halves and you will see an interesting situation. For while the '48-D has a lower mintage and is certainly not less rare, it has been rated as a lesser coin all the way along the line. I think this is due to the subconscious prejudice on the part of most collectors in favor of P-mint first year type coins. Even today, the Philadelphia mint coin sells for nearly 46% more, which is, perhaps, the best indication of how undervalued the latter actually is. A similar but more extreme situation formerly existed with respect to 1949, with the P-mint coin selling at five times the price of the Denver issue. At the present time, this inequity has been largely corrected.

Another Franklin half which I find to be currently underpriced is the 1953-P coin. With only 2.7 million struck, this item is one of the scarcest of the entire series, and certainly seems a bargain by comparison to the other leaders. The same holds true for the 1955 with its almost identical mintage.

Perhaps ever better buys are the 1956 and 1958-P halves, each with a mere 4 million mintage. To put the matter clearly before you, which would you rather own for the few dollars difference, a 1958-P or the common 1952-D?

Before closing my list, let me add what many of you will find a surprising recommendation, namely that you do not overlook the 1968-S, '69-S, '70-S and '70-D half dollars. For while the mintages of all of these cannot be considered as less than exorbitant, relatively few rolls were salted away. It will doubtless be awhile before this fact is properly appreciated, but the time will surely come.

I will conclude my predictions with a list of recommended issues and average increases that may be anticipated over the next two years. A number of issues which were not discussed in the foregoing section have been added, so the reader should go over it very carefully.

Cents		Dimes	
Date	**Anticipated Increase**	**Date**	**Anticipated Increase**
1936-S	15%	1946-D	25%
1937-S	30%	1946-S	50%
1938-S	20%	1947-P	25%
1939-D	50%	1949-D	50%
1941-S	25%	1949-S	25%
1943-S	25%	1950-S	20%
1946-S	200%	1951-S	50%
1954-S	25%	1952-S	20%
1955-S	50%	1953-S	25%
1955-D	100%	1954-S	30%
1960-P SD	35%	1955-P	40%
1960-D SD	100%	1955-D	50%
1967	50%	1955-S	60%
1970-S SD	50%	1958-P	100%

Nickels		Quarters	
1938-D Buff.	25%	1940-S	35%
1938-S	50%	1946-S	25%
1943-D	25%	1947-S	20%
1945-S	50%	1953-S	45%
1946-S	40%	1954-S	25%
1947-S	25%	1955-D	30%
1948-S	100%	1958-P	50%
1949-S	50%	Half Dollars	
1949-D	40%	1948-D	40%
1950-P	25%	1951-D	25%
1950-D	30%	1952-S	30%
1951-S	25%	1953-P	25%
1952-S	50%	1954-S	50%
1953-S	50%	1955-P	35%
1954-S	50%	1959-D	30%
1955-P	60%		

There remains some general advice to be given to the would-be investor. The first concerns the means by which he can determine when a new trend, upwards or downwards, is imminent. Of course, the most obvious way is to do as we have done, namely to analyze current prices by comparison to those of 1964 and so discover which issues are now underpriced. A second, and not less indispensable means, is to follow as closely as possible the buy and sell ads of the different dealers advertising in *Coin World, Numismatic News, CoinAge* etc. You might also supplement your reading with a subscription to the *Coin Dealer Newsletter,* which gives the averaged wholesale roll prices week by week. It is important to compare as many different ads as possible since dealers sometimes prepare their prices jointly, and will also frequently cite abnormally high or low prices on certain items for the purpose of influencing the market.

A good practice is to note in how many different ads each of the issues are being offered. Your data will provide you with good evidence for their predictable future. For example, if a particular issue has begun to climb and then suddenly disappears from the offerings, you will know that a substantial increase may be anticipated with its reappearance. At such a time you should make every effort to procure a quantity even if you have to pay what seems to you a bit of a premium. Again, if an item disappears after starting to decline, you can assume that, barring a general recession in rolls, the owners are simply not going to put it out again until the conditions are more favorable.

Don't overlook new issues, even if their mintage is substantial. Since you can obtain them at face value, you can never lose and the coins are bound to build up a premium.

The first rule then is to be alert. A smart investor will always be watching to see which way the wind is blowing and at what velocity. Remember that trends bear in themselves the means for further momentum, and every dollar you invest in an item contributes to its rise in value according to the law of inflation. Moreover, the fact that the market is bullish will itself induce the investment of new capital and so perpetuate its upward swing. Conversely, when money is withdrawn, the items find less of a market and so decline, which, in turn, discourages would-be investors. Even then, however, the slackening of interest in rolls will cause new issues to become scarce, and so eventually rekindle collector enthusiasm. As we have seen, this occurred in 1958.

The pessimist will point to the post-1964 decline as an indication of the dangers inherent in the roll market. But when we take a closer look, what real dangers were there? If you had begun collecting rolls in 1955 and kept them to the present time you would hardly have suffered financially. Of course, if you began investing in late 1964, you would not have fared so well. But then the handwriting was on the wall, and if, after six months or so you unloaded you would not have been seriously hurt. Certainly, much more has been lost in the stock market during a comparable period. The only persons who really felt the squeeze during the roll depression were the dealers who had acquired enormous stocks which they were unable to unload without altogether destroying the market and, perhaps in the process, their chief means of support. The average investor, having no such dependence, was free to sell as soon as he wished and, if he were not altogether asleep, he did so without further ado.

In any case, we shall not likely ever again have a situation like that of 1965 when the Treasury Department, with a desperate coin shortage looming, set about to break roll hoarding. It is true, of course, that the roll market, as well as numismatics generally, is susceptible to the general effects of recession; but then recessions come and go, and despite their unpleasant aspects they offer us a rare opportunity for good investment.

Finally, I would advise the investor to establish as friendly as possible a relationship with the dealers with whom he does business. Ask them their real opinion of this or that issue, then compare these opinions with one another as well as with your own findings. But remember, they have to be right most of the time;—their living depends on it.

RETAIL PRICE AVERAGES FOR UNC. CENT ROLLS*

Date	Mintage in Mills.	1940	1950	1954	1955	1956	1957	1958
1934	219.1	$1.90	$4.00	$6.00	$ 9.40	$13.50	$28.50	$34.00
1934-D	28.4	2.40	6.50	NA	25.00	28.50	75.00	90.00
1935	245.4	.85	2.15	5.00	7.50	7.55	16.75	19.25
1935-D	47.0	1.80	4.00	NA	18.00	18.00	37.50	27.50
1935-S	38.7	1.80	4.50	NA	18.00	18.00	NA	50.00
1936	309.6	.85	2.00	3.00	7.35	7.55	16.75	16.75
1936-D	40.6	1.80	2.00	5.75	7.55	7.55	16.50	19.50
1936-S	29.1	1.35	2.35	6.50	7.55	7.55	18.00	22.50
1937	309.2	1.10	1.25	2.30	3.50	4.50	9.50	12.65
1937-D	50.4	1.10	1.50	2.80	4.50	4.50	12.00	14.00
1937-S	34.5	1.10	1.50	3.00	7.50	7.50	16.50	16.50
1938	156.7	1.35	2.35	4.25	7.50	NA	37.50	37.50
1938-D	20.0	.95	2.35	NA	7.50	8.55	31.00	23.50
1938-S	15.2	.95	2.35	5.35	7.50	NA	40.00	35.00
1939	316.5	.85	1.25	2.50	4.50	4.50	11.50	12.50
1939-D	15.2	.95	3.35	7.75	15.00	NA	NA	69.00
1939-S	52.1	.95	1.50	3.85	9.50	9.55	21.00	18.00
1940	586.8	.80	1.50	2.25	3.50	NA	10.00	9.85
1940-D	81.4	.95	1.20	2.50	5.50	5.50	9.75	9.65
1940-S	112.9	.95	1.20	2.50	4.50	4.55	13.00	9.50
1941	887.0		.95	1.95	3.50	3.50	10.00	7.75
1941-D	128.7		.95	1.90	3.50	3.50	10.00	8.50
1941-S	92.4		1.25	2.50	5.35	5.55	8.25	9.65
1942	657.8		.85	1.00	1.00	2.65	2.75	5.00
1942-D	206.7		.85	1.00	1.00	2.35	2.75	5.00
1942-S	85.6		4.00	5.00	9.25	9.60	15.00	38.25
1943	684.6		.75	1.00	.95	3.50	4.50	5.50
1943-D	217.7		.75	1.05	.95	3.75	5.50	8.25
1943-S	191.6		1.90	3.50	7.40	NA	20.00	25.00
1944	1435.4		.80	.85	.85	1.75	1.75	3.15
1944-D	430.6		.80	.85	.85	1.75	1.75	3.15
1944-S	282.8		.80	.85	.85	2.25	2.10	4.30
1945	1040.5		.80	.85	.85	1.75	1.75	2.50
1945-D	226.3		.85	.85	.85	1.75	1.75	2.50
1945-S	181.8		.85	.85	.85	2.25	2.15	3.55

* Except for 1971, all figures represent end of year prices.

Date	Mintage in Mills.	1950	1954	1955	1956	1957	1958
1946	991.7	.75	.85	.85	1.70	1.75	2.50
1946-D	315.7	.75	.85	.85	1.70	1.75	2.50
1946-S	198.1	.75	.85	.85	2.20	2.20	3.50
1947	190.6	.75	2.90	2.50	3.80	3.85	NA
1947-D	194.8	.75	1.00	1.25	2.65	3.10	3.65
1947-S	99.0	.75	1.00	1.25	3.15	3.20	4.75
1948	317.6	.75	2.60	2.50	3.50	3.50	4.25
1948-D	172.6	.75	1.15	2.50	3.50	3.50	4.25
1948-S	81.7	.75	1.15	2.50	4.50	4.85	8.50
1949	217.5	.75	1.25	3.50	3.75	3.90	7.00
1949-D	154.4	75	3.50	3.50	3.75	3.90	5.15
1949-S	64.3	.75	3.50	3.65	5.50	11.00	17.50
1950	272.7	.75	2.50	2.25	2.75	3.25	4.50
1950-D	335.0	.75	1.00	2.25	2.50	2.75	3.50
1950-S	118.5	.75	1.00	2.25	2.65	3.25	10.00
1951	294.6		.90	.95	1.75	4.50	8.25
1951-D	625.4		.90	.95	1.50	1.75	2.75
1951-S	100.9		NA	3.50	3.80	7.50	12.50
1952	186.9		.90	.95	1.75	5.00	6.25
1952-D	746.1		.90	.95	.95	1.55	2.50
1952-S	137.8		1.50	2.45	2.80	3.75	6.50
1953	256.9		.75	.85	.95	1.25	1.75
1953-D	700.5		.75	.85	.95	1.25	1.75
1953-S	181.8		.75	1.25	2.25	2.75	4.50
1954	71.9		.70	1.25	1.50	1.85	7.50
1954-D	251.6		.70	.75	.85	1.00	1.50
1954-S	96.2		.70	.90	1.20	1.50	3.00
1955	331.0			.70	.95	1.25	1.65
1955-D	563.3			.70	.85	1.00	1.25
1955-S	44.6			1.40	1.65	1.80	4.75
1956	421.4				.70	.85	.95
1956-D	1098.2				.70	.85	.95
1957	283.8					.75	.85
1957-D	1051.3					.75	.85
1958	253.4						.75
1958-D	801.0						.75

Date	Mintage in Mills.	1959	1960	1961	1962	1963	1964	1965
1934	219.1	$ 47.50	$ 50.00	NA	NA	$170.00	$115.00	$ 95.00
1934-D	28.4	150.00	155.00	NA	375.00	600.00	NA	395.00
1935	245.4	23.75	27.50	NA	NA	55.00	46.00	38.00
1935-D	47.0	32.50	35.00	NA	80.00	175.00	115.00	75.00

Date	Mintage in Mills.	1959	1960	1961	1962	1963	1964	1965
1935-S	38.7	NA	55.00	NA	145.00	285.00	200.00	150.00
1936	309.6	18.00	22.50	28.00	28.00	35.00	30.00	22.00
1936-D	40.6	22.50	24.00	29.50	NA	120.00	85.00	65.00
1936-S	29.1	32.00	37.50	39.50	65.00	180.00	110.00	85.00
1937	309.2	15.00	16.00	18.00	21.00	35.00	28.50	20.00
1937-D	50.4	15.25	17.50	18.00	22.50	55.00	45.00	40.00
1937-S	34.5	22.50	20.00	22.50	NA	125.00	80.00	62.50
1938	156.7	40.00	40.00	35.00	39.50	75.00	48.00	41.00
1938-D	20.0	29.50	29.50	29.50	55.00	150.00	125.00	110.00
1938-S	15.2	40.00	42.50	65.00	125.00	215.00	172.50	120.00
1939	316.5	17.00	14.00	16.00	21.00	30.00	25.00	20.00
1939-D	15.2	85.00	95.00	130.00	NA	275.00	217.50	180.00
1939-S	52.1	22.00	20.50	20.50	31.00	75.00	60.00	37.50
1940	586.8	15.00	15.00	18.50	25.00	32.50	26.00	22.50
1940-D	81.4	17.50	15.00	19.00	25.00	55.00	47.50	40.00
1940-S	112.9	15.00	14.75	18.50	24.25	40.00	35.00	22.50
1941	887.0	15.00	14.50	20.00	25.00	32.50	29.00	24.00
1941-D	128.7	17.00	15.00	20.00	35.00	70.00	55.00	43.00
1941-S	92.4	17.50	17.00	21.00	45.00	65.00	57.50	38.00
1942	657.8	10.75	11.50	10.00	12.00	15.00	18.25	10.50
1942-D	206.7	9.50	8.50	7.50	11.75	18.75	21.00	14.00
1942-S	85.6	42.00	40.00	65.00	120.00	212.50	210.00	182.50
1943	684.6	9.00	7.00	7.25	.8.00	11.50	12.50	11.50
1943-D	217.7	12.35	8.50	10.00	10.50	25.00	26.00	20.00
1943-S	191.6	36.00	30.00	29.50	37.00	47.50	55.00	40.00
1944	1435.4	7.50	8.00	5.50	8.00	9.00	12.00	8.50
1944-D	430.6	7.50	8.00	5.50	7.00	12.00	14.00	9.00
1944-S	282.8	10.00	9.50	8.00	13.00	19.00	22.50	15.00
1945	1040.5	15.50	14.00	9.75	10.25	10.75	15.00	12.00
1945-D	226.3	11.00	8.50	6.25	7.50	19.00	21.50	12.50
1945-S	181.8	8.50	8.75	7.75	13.00	18.50	23.50	16.00
1946	991.7	6.25	8.00	5.00	6.00	9.00	9.50	7.75
1946-D	315.7	6.25	9.00	5.00	6.00	12.50	18.00	13.00
1946-S	198.1	6.90	7.50	6.75	13.00	17.00	18.50	12.00
1947	190.6	27.50	25.00	21.00	22.50	30.00	33.50	21.00
1947-D	194.8	10.50	9.00	7.25	10.00	15.00	15.50	10.25
1947-S	99.0	12.50	11.50	8.50	19.00	47.50	45.00	26.75
1948	317.6	16.50	18.25	15.50	15.50	17.00	16.25	13.00
1948-D	172.6	11.50	9.75	9.00	10.00	18.35	15.50	13.00
1948-S	81.7	15.00	18.50	17.50	24.00	60.00	75.00	52.00
1949	217.5	24.00	22.00	17.50	24.50	29.50	29.00	17.75
1949-D	154.4	10.25	12.50	8.00	16.25	32.25	27.00	18.00
1949-S	64.3	45.00	29.00	33.50	42.50	70.00	83.50	70.00

Date	Mintage in Mills.	1959	1960	1961	1962	1963	1964	1965
1950	272.7	16.50	13.50	13.50	16.25	18.25	16.00	11.50
1950-D	335.0	9.00	8.25	8.75	9.50	9.50	9.75	7.75
1950-S	118.5	16.00	17.75	21.00	25.00	29.00	35.50	32.25
1951	294.6	18.50	17.75	17.75	21.00	24.25	30.00	19.00
1951-D	625.4	8.25	7.50	5.50	6.00	6.50	7.50	4.75
1951-S	100.9	25.00	22.00	24.50	37.50	55.00	56.00	39.25
1952	186.9	14.25	14.50	16.50	16.50	29.00	28.00	27.00
1952-D	746.1	6.50	6.50	5.00	5.00	5.00	6.50	4.35
1952-S	137.8	20.00	17.50	19.25	24.25	28.50	37.50	24.50
1953	256.9	8.50	7.00	5.50	7.00	7.50	10.00	8.50
1953-D	700.5	6.50	5.75	4.50	5.00	6.50	5.35	4.00
1953-S	181.8	12.50	10.50	11.50	19.50	25.75	25.00	18.75
1954	71.9	16.50	10.00	13.25	27.50	32.00	36.00	27.00
1954-D	251.6	5.50	5.35	4.25	4.50	8.00	7.50	5.50
1954-S	96.2	7.00	6.00	7.25	18.00	24.50	22.00	14.50
1955	331.0	5.50	5.25	5.25	5.50	8.00	7.50	5.25
1955-D	563.3	4.40	4.35	4.00	4.50	8.50	7.25	4.50
1955-S	44.6	9.00	8.25	12.50	35.00	40.00	35.50	26.00
1956	421.4	3.30	4.25	3.00	3.00	6.25	4.85	4.35
1956-D	1098.2	3.20	2.50	2.10	2.25	3.00	2.50	1.65
1957	283.8	2.35	3.00	2.55	2.75	5.65	4.85	3.75
1957-D	1051.3	2.25	2.25	1.65	1.75	2.00	2.00	1.55
1958	253.4	1.35	2.35	2.15	2.50	7.00	5.00	3.35
1958-D	801.0	1.05	1.50	1.25	1.50	2.10	2.10	1.35
1959	610.9	.75	1.40	.95	1.15	2.85	2.25	1.25
1959-D	1279.8	.75	1.15	.95	1.10	2.00	1.75	1.00
1960	588.1		.90	.75				
1960 SD			200.00		152.50	400.00	367.50	282.50
1960-D	1580.9		.75	.75	NA	1.45	1.40	1.10
1960-D SD			5.00	4.85	NA	20.00	17.50	15.00
1961	756.4			.75	.85	1.25	1.50	1.00
1961-D	1753.3			.75	.85	1.10	1.25	1.00
1962	609.3				.80	1.10	1.45	1.25
1962-D	1793.1				.75	.90	1.10	.95
1963	757.2					.85	.85	1.00
1963-D	1774.0					.80	.85	.95
1964	2652.6						.75	.95
1964-D	3799.1						.75	.95

Date	Mintage in Mills.	1966	1967	1968	1969	Aug. 1971
1934	219.1	NA	$ 50.00	$ 60.00	$ 50.00	$ 40.00
1934-D	28.4	NA	210.00	235.00	245.00	215.00
1935	245.4	$ 26.00	27.00	34.50	35.00	24.50
1935-D	47.0	57.50	42.50	46.50	37.00	25.00
1935-S	38.7	125.00	86.00	100.00	75.00	60.00
1936	309.6	18.00	23.50	31.00	24.00	19.00
1936-D	40.6	47.50	38.50	43.50	34.50	21.00
1936-S	29.1	62.50	57.00	57.50	34.00	26.50
1937	309.2	17.00	18.50	25.00	23.50	19.00
1937-D	50.4	28.00	29.00	33.50	23.00	17.00
1937-S	34.5	40.00	32.00	36.00	25.00	18.00
1938	156.7	35.00	34.50	35.00	26.50	17.00
1938-D	20.0	85.00	57.50	58.00	40.00	31.50
1938-S	15.2	90.00	67.50	71.00	68.00	37.50
1939	316.5	15.75	19.50	24.00	18.00	12.50
1939-D	15.2	115.00	110.00	130.00	95.00	65.00
1939-S	52.1	28.00	24.00	27.50	21.50	16.00
1940	586.8	14.50	14.00	14.50	11.50	8.50
1940-D	81.4	25.00	22.50	23.00	18.50	15.00
1940-S	112.9	15.00	14.00	16.00	12.25	11.00
1941	887.0	15.00	13.00	17.50	15.50	11.00
1941-D	128.7	25.00	29.00	38.00	35.00	32.50
1941-S	92.4	25.00	29.00	38.00	35.50	37.50
1942	657.8	7.00	7.00	9.00	8.00	6.00
1942-D	206.7	9.00	8.50	9.00	8.00	6.00
1942-S	85.8	105.00	100.00	120.00	105.00	75.00
1943	684.6	9.00	8.00	8.50	6.50	6.00
1943-D	217.7	17.00	15.50	18.00	14.50	10.00
1943-S	191.6	30.00	29.50	34.00	25.00	25.00
1944	1435.4	5.50	5.25	5.50	4.00	4.00
1944-D	430.6	6.00	6.00	6.50	3.75	3.50
1944-S	282.8	7.50	7.25	8.50	6.75	6.50
1945	1040.5	7.50	7.00	8.50	7.50	6.50
1945-D	226.3	7.00	6.75	8.50	7.00	6.50
1945-S	181.8	9.50	8.75	8.50	8.00	6.50
1946	991.7	5.35	4.80	6.25	4.25	2.50
1946-D	315.7	6.00	5.85	7.00	4.25	3.50
1946-S	198.1	6.00	5.50	7.25	4.25	3.25
1947	190.6	14.50	14.50	17.00	14.50	11.50
1947-D	194.8	6.25	5.25	6.50	5.75	4.75
1947-S	99.0	14.35	14.00	15.50	17.50	17.00
1948	317.6	7.75	8.00	10.00	9.50	8.00
1948-D	172.6	7.50	7.00	6.75	5.85	4.50

Date	Mintage in Mills.	1966	1967	1968	1969	Aug. 1971
1948-S	81.7	31.50	27.50	29.50	23.00	16.50
1949	217.5	12.00	12.00	14.25	12.65	10.00
1949-D	154.4	10.00	10.00	11.85	8.50	7.00
1949-S	64.3	35.00	34.50	40.00	29.00	22.00
1950	272.7	6.00	7.50	12.00	13.35	7.50
1950-D	335.0	5.75	4.50	5.35	4.85	3.00
1950-S	118.5	18.00	15.50	15.65	14.00	10.00
1951	294.6	15.00	14.00	17.00	14.50	13.00
1951-D	625.4	3.75	3.50	4.15	3.50	2.00
1951-S	100.9	20.50	18.50	25.65	22.75	13.50
1952	186.9	16.00	14.00	15.00	13.25	12.00
1952-D	746.1	3.35	3.00	2.85	2.50	1.75
1952-S	137.8	16.00	14.50	15.75	14.35	11.00
1953	256.9	6.00	5.50	6.35	4.75	3.50
1953-D	700.5	3.15	2.65	2.75	2.50	1.75
1953-S	181.8	10.35	8.75	8.00	6.00	5.00
1954	71.9	21.50	14.00	16.50	12.50	9.00
1954-D	251.6	3.25	3.00	3.00	2.50	2.50
1954-S	96.2	7.75	7.25	7.25	5.65	3.50
1955	331.0	3.50	3.50	4.25	3.65	2.50
1955-D	563.3	3.25	3.00	2.50	1.75	1.00
1955-S	44.6	19.00	17.00	15.35	12.35	9.50
1956	421.4	4.00	3.50	2.85	1.65	1.25
1956-D	1098.2	1.25	1.25	1.25	1.00	.75
1957	283.8	3.35	3.00	2.35	1.35	1.25
1957-D	1051.3	1.15	1.00	1.00	.90	.75
1958	253.4	2.75	2.75	2.25	1.55	1.00
1958-D	801.0	1.15	1.15	1.00	1.00	.80
1959	610.9	1.25	1.25	.95	.95	.85
1959-D	1279.8	1.00	1.00	.95	1.00	.85
1960	588.1	1.00	1.00	.90	.90	.85
1960 SD		180.00	170.00	162.50	150.00	105.00
1960-D	1580.9	1.00	1.00		.90	.85
1960-D SD		7.50	7.50	5.50	3.75	2.50
1961	756.4	1.00	1.00	1.00	.90	.85
1961-D	1753.3	1.00	1.00	1.00	.85	.80
1962	609.3	1.00	1.00	1.00	.85	.85
1962-D	1793.1	.95	.90	1.00	.80	.80
1963	757.2	.90	.90	.90	.85	.80
1963-D	1774.0	.75	.75	.90	.85	.80
1964	2652.6	.75	.75	1.00	.85	.85
1964-D	3799.1	.75	.75	1.00	.95	.95
1965	1497.2				.95	1.00

Date	Mintage in Mills.	1958	1969	Aug. 1971
1966	2188.1		.95	1.00
1967	3048.7	.85	.95	1.00
1968	1707.9	.90	.85	1.00
1968-D	2886.3	.90	.85	.85
1968-S	261.3	.95	1.00	1.00
1969	1136.9		.80	.80
1969-D	4002.8		.80	.80
1969-S	547.3		.85	.85
1970				.85
1970-D				.80
1970-S				1.00
1970-S SD				52.50

RETAIL PRICE AVERAGES FOR UNC. FIVE-CENT ROLLS

Date	Mintage in Mills.	1955	1963	1964	Aug. 1971
1938	19.5	$ 6.80	$110.00	$115.00	$ 23.50
1938-D	5.4	18.00	395.00	300.00	120.00
1938-S	4.1	19.50	425.00	395.00	135.00
1939	120.6	27.50	82.50	65.00	23.00
1939-D	3.5	NA	NA	NA	850.00
1939-S	6.6	135.00	725.00	595.00	275.00
1940	176.5	7.50	30.00	40.00	15.00
1940-D	43.5	15.00	51.00	55.00	19.50
1940-S	39.7	15.00	90.00	90.00	40.00
1941	203.3	6.35	25.00	35.00	15.00
1941-D	53.4	6.35	45.00	49.00	18.50
1941-S	43.4	6.35	65.00	62.50	25.00
1942 (I)	49.8	5.35	107.50	90.00	30.00
1942 (II)	57.9	3.50	350.00	370.00	145.00
1942-D	13.9	42.50	700.00	520.00	200.00
1942-S	32.9	3.50	150.00	167.50	79.50
1943	271.2	3.35	72.50	73.50	27.50
1943-D	15.3	3.35	150.00	170.00	65.00
1943-S	104.1	3.35	65.00	55.00	26.00
1944	119.2	2.75	95.00	117.50	36.00
1944-D	32.3	2.75	82.50	80.00	57.50
1944-S	21.6	2.75	96.50	142.50	60.00
1945	119.4	2.75	70.00	117.50	55.00
1945-D	37.2	2.75	61.00	65.00	37.00
1945-S	58.9	2.75	57.50	55.00	25.00
1946	161.1	2.75	16.75	20.00	6.00

Date	Mintage in mills.	1955	1963	1964	Aug. 1971
1946-D	45.3	2.75	25.00	40.00	24.00
1946-S	13.6	4.25	76.50	78.00	24.50
1947	95.0	2.75	18.50	21.00	6.00
1947-D	37.8	2.75	29.50	43.50	16.00
1947-S	24.7	2.75	85.00	95.00	16.00
1948	89.3	3.50	17.50	22.50	6.50
1948-D	44.7	3.50	62.50	72.50	30.00
1948-S	11.3	3.50	90.00	115.00	23.00
1949	60.7	4.25	40.00	48.00	12.00
1949-D	36.5	4.35	40.00	60.00	22.50
1949-S	9.7	9.50	142.50	165.00	42.50
1950	9.8	11.50	193.50	180.00	42.50
1950-D	2.6	9.50	790.00	925.00	315.00
1951	28.6	2.50	63.50	62.50	17.50
1951-D	20.5	7.50	110.00	90.00	29.00
1951-S	7.8	14.75	250.00	325.00	60.00
1952	64.0	2.65	23.75	20.00	9.50
1952-D	30.6	3.15	140.00	190.00	40.00
1952-S	20.6	2.65	57.50	50.00	15.00
1953	46.6	2.65	17.00	17.00	4.00
1953-D	59.9	2.65	23.00	21.00	6.00
1953-S	19.2	2.90	50.00	47.50	12.00
1954	47.7	2.90	17.50	14.00	4.00
1954-D	117.1	2.50	13.25	8.00	4.00
1954-S	29.4	2.65	25.00	22.00	4.00
1955	7.9	2.30	145.00	125.00	25.00
1955-D	74.5	2.45	27.50	20.00	4.00
1956	35.2		13.25	11.00	4.00
1956-D	67.2		12.00	8.00	3.00
1957	38.4		14.50	14.50	4.00
1957-D	136.8		6.50	4.50	2.75
1958	17.1		35.00	37.00	6.50
1958-D	168.2		6.00	4.00	2.75
1959	27.2		14.00	12.50	3.25
1959-D	160.7		4.00	3.00	2.75
1960	55.4		6.00	4.75	2.75
1960-D	192.6		4.50	3.25	2.75
1961	73.6		4.50	4.25	2.75
1961-D	229.3		4.50	3.25	2.75
1962	97.4		3.50	3.35	2.75
1962-D	280.2		3.50	3.00	2.75
1963	175.8		2.75	3.00	2.75
1963-D	276.8		2.65	2.75	2.75

RETAIL PRICE AVERAGES FOR UNC. DIME ROLLS

Date	Mintage in Mills.	1955	1963	1964	Aug. 1971
1946	255.3	$ 12.25	$ 22.50	$ 20.00	$ 13.50
1946-D	61.0	12.25	25.00	50.00	16.50
1946-S	27.9	13.75	62.50	92.50	22.50
1947	121.5	23.50	112.50	68.00	19.00
1947-D	46.8	25.00	47.50	61.00	34.50
1947-S	34.8	25.00	70.00	80.00	22.50
1948	75.00	29.50	202.50	127.50	42.50
1948-D	52.8	27.50	45.00	67.50	32.50
1948-S	35.5	27.50	77.50	93.50	35.00
1949	30.9	30.00	490.00	470.00	215.00
1949-D	26.0	14.50	113.50	145.00	85.00
1949-S	13.5	120.00	800.00	690.00	425.00
1950	50.1	29.75	115.00	95.00	60.00
1950-D	46.8	15.00	32.00	N.A.	75.00
1950-S	20.4	90.00	615.00	570.00	190.00
1951	102.9	9.50	100.00	80.00	29.00
1951-D	56.5	9.50	46.50	60.00	23.50
1951-S	31.6	80.00	590.00	490.00	125.00
1952	99.0	6.75	27.50	28.50	17.50
1952-D	122.1	6.50	22.50	22.50	20.00
1952-S	44.4	26.50	195.00	135.00	50.00
1953	53.5	6.25	67.50	45.00	18.00
1953-D	136.4	6.25	19.00	18.00	10.00
1953S	39.2	7.50	42.50	47.50	16.00
1954	114.0	5.90	12.00	13.50	8.00
1954-D	106.4	5.90	12.00	13.50	8.50
1954-S	22.9	6.50	45.00	47.50	16.50
1955	12.5	5.70	92.50	127.50	31.00
1955-D	14.0	7.00	65.00	75.00	18.00
1955-S	18.6	6.50	67.50	52.50	13.50
1956	108.6		9.70	12.35	8.50
1956-D	108.0		9.00	10.00	8.50
1957	160.2		9.00	9.75	8.00
1957-D	113.4		8.25	11.00	20.00
1958	31.9		32.50	40.00	12.00
1958-D	136.6		8.00	8.00	7.50
1959	85.8		9.00	9.35	7.50
1959-D	164.9		7.65	8.65	7.50
1960	70.4		10.00	9.50	7.50
1960-D	200.2		8.25	7.50	7.50
1961	93.7		17.50	12.00	7.50

Date	Mintage in Mills.	1963	1964	Aug. 1971
1961-D	209.1	7.00	6.85	7.50
1962	72.5	8.35	8.25	7.50
1962-D	334.9	7.00	6.75	7.00
1963	123.7	6.35	6.50	7.00
1963-D	421.5	6.00	6.25	7.00

RETAIL PRICE AVERAGES FOR
UNC. QUARTER DOLLAR ROLLS

Date	Mintage in Mills.	1955	1963	1964	Aug. 1971
1940	35.7	$ 82.50	$ 275.00	$ 300.00	$125.00
1940-D	2.8	125.00	1125.00	1750.00	950.00
1940-S	8.2	40.00	130.00	275.00	160.00
1941	79.0	16.00	45.00	105.00	42.50
1941-D	16.7	31.75	115.00	195.00	200.00
1941-S	16.0	40.00	120.00	250.00	200.00
1942	102.1	13.75	73.50	93.00	35.00
1942-D	17.5	13.00	50.00	95.00	90.00
1942-S	19.4	55.00	307.50	760.00	550.00
1943	99.7	13.25	29.00	55.00	65.00
1943-D	16.1	15.00	42.00	145.00	92.50
1943-S	21.7	40.00	117.50	225.00	150.00
1944	105.0	12.50	35.00	50.00	37.50
1944-D	14.6	12.50	54.00	150.00	76.00
1944-S	12.6	12.50	53.00	110.00	62.50
1945	74.4	12.50	25.00	45.00	27.50
1945-D	12.3	12.50	35.00	85.00	65.00
1945-S	17.0	12.50	35.00	80.00	46.00
1946	53.4	12.00	25.00	45.00	33.50
1946-D	9.1	12.50	45.00	150.00	62.50
1946-S	4.2	12.50	102.50	162.50	80.00
1947	22.6	12.50	30.00	75.00	41.50
1947-D	15.3	12.50	30.00	75.00	41.50
1947-S	5.5	12.50	72.00	185.00	75.00
1948	35.2	12.50	27.50	45.00	27.00
1948-D	16.8	12.75	29.00	65.00	60.00
1948-S	16.0	13.25	37.50	65.00	38.50
1949	9.3	15.00	327.50	492.50	240.00
1949-D	10.1	12.75	75.00	112.50	90.00
1950	24.9	14.75	85.00	65.00	32.50
1950-D	21.1	12.50	26.00	50.00	32.50

Date	Mintage in Mills.	1955	1963	1964	Aug. 1971
1950-S	10.3	16.50	83.50	153.00	72.00
1951	34.4	17.50	22.00	43.50	24.00
1951-D	35.4	12.50	19.00	40.00	29.00
1951-S	9.1	25.00	120.00	275.00	175.00
1952	38.8	12.50	19.65	35.00	19.50
1952-D	49.8	12.50	18.65	32.00	23.00
1952-S	13.7	14.50	48.00	130.00	59.00
1953	18.7	12.00	90.00	90.00	51.00
1953-D	56.1	11.75	16.00	22.50	18.00
1953-S	14.0	11.75	35.00	52.00	35.00
1954	54.4	11.25	15.50	19.50	15.75
1954-D	42.3	11.25	47.50	30.00	15.75
1954-S	11.8	12.00	35.00	52.50	23.00
1955	18.2	10.75	45.00	53.00	22.00
1955-D	3.2		145.00	160.00	79.00
1956	44.1		14.25	17.50	16.00
1956-D	32.3		17.00	22.50	16.00
1957	46.5		15.00	15.00	14.50
1957-D	77.9		14.50	15.00	14.50
1958	6.4		43.00	73.00	34.00
1958-D	78.1		13.50	14.35	15.00
1959	24.4		13.00	18.25	15.00
1959-D	62.1		13.50	13.75	15.00
1960	29.2		13.00	15.50	15.00
1960-D	63.0		12.50	14.25	14.50
1961	37.0		13.75	13.75	14.50
1961-D	83.7		13.75	13.75	14.00
1962	36.2		13.75	13.75	14.00
1962-D	127.6		13.75	13.50	14.00
1963	74.3		11.85	12.25	14.00
1963-D	135.3		11.65	12.25	14.00

RETAIL PRICE AVERAGES FOR UNC. HALF DOLLAR ROLLS

Date	Mintage in Mills.	1955	1963	1964	Aug. 1971
1948	3.0	$45.00	$115.00	$190.00	$115.00
1948-D	2.0	18.75	55.00	105.00	62.00
1949	5.6	NA	500.00	620.00	290.00
1949-D	4.1	21.50	125.00	200.00	240.00
1949-S	3.7	25.00	175.00	400.00	250.00
1950	7.7	21.50	195.00	300.00	165.00

Date	Mintage in Mills.	1955	1963	1964	Aug. 1971
1950-D	8.0	21.50	110.00	195.00	135.00
1951	16.8	17.50	60.00	75.00	67.00
1951-D	8.5	17.50	62.50	175.00	215.00
1951-S	13.7	25.00	85.00	170.00	115.00
1952	21.2	12.25	32.50	90.00	37.50
1952-D	25.4	12.25	27.50	32.50	27.00
1952-S	5.5	15.50	67.50	157.50	125.00
1953	2.7	15.00	80.00	230.00	135.00
1953-D	20.9	11.75	25.00	26.00	27.00
1953-S	4.1	11.75	30.00	80.00	63.00
1954	13.2	11.00	17.50	32.50	19.00
1954-D	25.4	11.15	21.50	24.00	19.00
1954-S	5.0	13.50	29.00	57.50	33.00
1955	2.5		43.50	187.50	115.00
1956	4.0		22.50	65.00	42.00
1957	5.1		17.50	45.00	32.00
1957-D	20.0		16.75	19.00	18.00
1958	4.0		24.50	60.00	32.00
1958-D	24.0		15.00	18.00	17.50
1959	6.2		16.00	32.00	22.50
1959-D	13.0		23.50	23.00	26.50
1960	6.0		15.00	28.00	21.00
1960-D	18.2		14.50	21.00	20.00
1961	8.3		16.75	24.00	19.00
1961-D	20.3		16.75	22.00	18.00
1962	9.7		14.00	20.00	18.00
1962-D	35.5		14.00	14.00	16.00
1963	22.2		12.00	14.50	15.00
1963-D	67.1		11.65	13.50	14.50

Chapter 4

How to Profit with
Proof and Commemorative Coins

Since proof and commemorative coins are the only series' intended especially for collectors and widely purchased by persons who otherwise have little interest in numismatics, they may be appropriately considered in the same chapter.

It is now known that proof coins have been struck, at least on special occasions, ever since the opening of the Philadelphia Mint in 1792. In the *Comprehensive Catalogue*, Mr. Taxay has discussed at length the history of these interesting pieces, describing the various changes they underwent at different periods and in different series'. Sets of proof coins were first issued by the Mint for collectors in 1858, and continued to be made through 1916, when, as a result of the changeover from brilliant to matte and sandblast finishes, collector interest seems to have largely fallen off. Sets of the old brilliant type were resumed in 1936, and when the great speculative boom hit numismatics in the mid 1950's, they were among the hottest items.

I have already described how, in 1965, to solve the growing coin shortage, the Treasury Department removed mintmarks from the coins thereby breaking the back of the roll market. Whatever justification this action may have had, there was certainly none at all for the simultaneous suspension of proof sets. Considering that these coins were not intended for circulation, and that the striking of a few million sets per year was not a great burden on the Mint, the suspension can only be construed as a punitive measure aimed at those who dealt primarily in modern U.S. coins.

As things turned out, however the additional penalty wasn't all that necessary. For with the decline of the roll market, that of the single coins, and by extension all other modern and semi-modern U.S. series', had inevitably to suffer. The extent to which proof sets themselves depreciated can be seen by the tabular figures given in this chapter. Their recovery, following resumption of the sets in 1968, should also be noted, together with the 1971 prices for these latter years. It would seem that today, as always, there is no better investment than current year proof sets purchased directly from the Mint. The older sets have also considerably recovered so that the series as a whole now stands just a little worse than it did in 1963. Doubtless it will continue to show gains, and should not be overlooked for a moderate investment.

When we compare the 1964 vs. 1970 performance of the older single proofs, we come up with some interesting statistics. The first group under consideration will be the minor coins. Prices for the cent and two-cent pieces have been collated from the *Numismatic Scrapbook Magazine,* those for the nickel three and five-cent pieces from auctions held by Stacks of New York City.

		1964	1970
1¢	1865	$285.00	$210.00
	1879	72.50	50.00
	1880	60.00	45.00
	1881	70.00	45.00
	1883	55.00	37.50
	1884	65.00	50.00
	1889	57.50	43.00
	1900-07	55.00	35.00
2¢	1868	135.00	82.50
	1870	105.00	75.00
	1872	195.00	135.00
	1873	645.00	400.00

		1964	1970
3¢	1877	640.00	375.00
	1878	135.00	115.00
	1879	38.00	37.50
	1880	40.00	37.50
	1881	45.00	31.50
	1882	40.00	34.00
	1887/6	195.00	180.00

		1964	1970
5¢	1871	$220.00	$160.00
	1875	125.00	90.00
	1876	50.00	42.00
	1878	210.00	130.00
	1879	67.50	57.50
	1881	52.00	50.00
	1884	51.00	37.50
	1885	365.00	190.00
	1890	44.00	30.00
	1895	55.00	30.00
	1896	130.00	57.50

It is clear both from the *Scrapbook* and Stacks prices that minor proof coins have lost considerable ground. Percentage-wise these series' would seem to be down on the average by about 25-33%. The auction figures are, of course, the more variable as we should expect. For the general rule among collectors is to bid only on what they themselves both need and can afford. On occasion this may result in an immoderately high price. On the other hand, what they pass up is naturally purchased by dealers at a somewhat depressed figure.

Now let's turn to the silver issues. In the absence of a large number of comparable prices, I can only give my general impression with regard to half dimes, which is that they have done very well for themselves. On the whole, I would calculate their gains at between 50 and 75%. The same holds for the seated liberty dimes, as we may see from the following *Scrapbook* prices.

		1964	1970
10¢	1870	$47.50	$69.00
	1875	45.00	63.00
	1876	40.00	58.00
	1882	40.00	58.00
	1883	40.00	69.50
	1886	40.00	69.50

By contrast, the Barber dimes have only held their own. For example, we find the following in the *Scrapbook*:

		1964	1970
10¢	1911	$ 80.00	$ 80.00
	1912	80.00	83.00
	1913	115.00	120.00

The Stacks sales tell a similar story:

	1964	1970
1894	55.00	60.00
1905	70.00	67.50
1909	65.00	65.00

In their infrequent appearances, the twenty-cent pieces seem likewise to have made but little headway since the 1964 period. The same may be said of the quarters, seated Libertys included, and this in my judgment is one of the more curious statistics.

Very definite and consistent gains are found among both the seated Liberty and Barber half dollar proofs. Once again, quoting from Stacks sales:

		1964	1970
50¢	1867	$90.00	$100.00
	1868	90.00	125.00
	1872	70.00	90.00
	1878	87.50	110.00
	1881	71.00	100.00
	1888	120.00	120.00
	1889	95.00	121.00
	1894	85.00	130.00
	1895	92.50	120.00
	1899	82.50	130.00
	1907	85.00	125.00

Like the half dollar proofs, those of the silver dollars and trade dollars seem to be up by about a third. Again, from Stacks:

		1964	1970
Silver $1	1862	$250.00	$360.00
	1871	170.00	275.00
	1878 8F	250.00	240.00
	1882	130.00	175.00
	1886	100.00	180.00
	1899	135.00	190.00
Trade $1	1874	320.00	340.00
	1878	370.00	470.00
	1883	350.00	450.00

With respect to gold proofs, our best basis for comparison will be 1964 Scrapbook prices as against the listings in the *Comprehensive Catalogue*. Accordingly:

		1964	1970
$1	1859	$415.00	$ 850.00
	1861	315.00	650.00
	1862	350.00	650.00
	1863	385.00	900.00
	1864	395.00	1,000.00
	1876	295.00	550.00
	1880	345.00	600.00
$2½	1891	$335.00	$600.00
	1894	495.00	700.00
	1899	290.00	475.00
	1900	295.00	425.00
$3	1886	$1,050.00 (gem)	$1,450.00
	1904	295.00	435.00

This much will suffice to show what gold proofs of all denominations have been doing in the last six or seven years. It should be noted, however, by way of warning, that the number of collectors of gold proofs are still comparatively few, and that those issues which are not the object of competitive bidding at auctions tend to do rather rather poorly by comparison to those that are. It is for this reason, as well as the poverty of current sell advertisements in the current NSM that I have chosen to compare the old listings with those of a current catalogue.

The reader will have noticed the markedly different performance between proofs of the minor coins and those of the silver and gold issues. I suspect that this is largely due to the removal of silver from the coinage in 1965 and our consequent preoccupation with the precious metals. Eventually, collectors will begin to realize how underpriced the former have become, and they will then rise very quickly.

To summarize, the following suggestions are given: Minor proofs, and especially the shield nickels, represent a good long-term investment. Among the silver coins, quarters, half dollars and silver dollars are the best picks, quarters because they are currently depressed, and half dollars and silver dollars because an anticipated rise in the price of the regular issues is bound to force up that of the proofs. Gold will probably move a little slower now, and will not yield sufficient profits for those whose main interest is investment.

AVERAGE RETAIL PRICES FOR PROOF SETS AS PER END OF YEAR

Date	Mintage	1955	1963	1964	Aug. 1971
1936	3,837	N.A.	$550.00	$1,250.00	$850.00
1937	5,542	$ 70.00	270.00	450.00	250.00
1938	8,045	42.00	130.00	240.00	145.00
1939	8,795	40.00	115.00	220.00	120.00
1940	11,246	30.00	97.50	140.00	100.00
1941	15,287	25.00	82.50	125.00	89.50
1942 (II)	21,120	25.00	79.00	145.00	115.00
1950	51,386	35.00	132.50	195.00	95.00
1951	57,500	22.50	69.00	105.00	60.00
1952	81,980	12.00	43.00	70.00	45.00
1953	128,800	6.00	27.50	49.00	28.50
1954	233,300	4.50	20.75	36.00	14.50
1955	378,200		19.25	42.00	19.50
1956	669,384		10.80	17.50	8.50
1957	1,247,952		7.00	12.50	5.00

Date	Mintage	1963	1964	1971
1958	875,652	11.00	22.00	11.00
1959	1,149,291	5.75	13.25	6.00
1960	1,691,602	5.60	9.00	5.00
1960 S.D.		51.00	48.00	18.50
1961	3,028,244	3.55	7.00	4.00
1962	3,218,019	3.50	7.00	4.00
1963	3,075,645	3.75	8.50	4.25
1964	3,950,762		15.00	5.00
1968-S	3,041,506			6.50
1969-S				5.50
1970-S				9.00
1971-S				6.00

Commemorative coins are a rather recent addition to the Mint's issues, having been struck for the first time in 1892. They are most obviously distinguished by the variety and memorial character of their designs. Traditionally, these coins have been issued at the instigation of some municipal, state or private group, which was allowed to purchase the emission at face value and then distribute it, at a profit, to the collecting community. In time, this practice degenerated into an outright subsidy, and the issue of commemoratives was suspended by the Government.

When we examine the progress of the commemorative coin market, a number of facts become apparent. The first is that the series as a whole, though continuously popular, has never been the object of such widespread speculation as were rolls and modern proof sets. Nevertheless, like most of the other modern U.S. coins, commemoratives, or at least a good many of them, have also declined somewhat since 1964.

If you will take a good look at the tabular figures, you will note that while almost every high-priced coin has dropped from its peak price, a number of the commoner ones show gains. This is the result of two things, first, the sale by many of the older collectors of their sets, and, secondly, the fact that a new group of collectors has warmed up to the series. Those who sold, owned, for the most part, complete or nearly complete sets, which, in itself, would have caused the market to decline more or less uniformly. But the new collectors, as always, have begun with the commoner issues, causing them to increase disproportionately to the rest.

It might be thought that the decline in the higher priced issues is the result of speculation. However, this can be easily disproved. First of all, many of these rarities increased by no more than 300% from 1955 to 1964, which is on the lower side of the average. Again, those issues which have indeed been subject to speculative hoarding, and which have shown the largest gains from 1955 to 1964, declined subsequently no more than the others, and for the simple reason that they were never unloaded.

The mintages given for the various issues represent the total struck minus those melted down before distribution was complete. However, a substantial portion of the early commemoratives were placed in circulation and eventually returned for redemption. This is one reason why they continue to realize higher prices than their mintages would seem to justify. Others, like the Hawaiian, are unduly rare because of hoarding. Knowing the individuals involved, however, I can foresee little chance that these issues will ever be unloaded in such quantities as to endanger their market value.

The first commemorative which looks good to me is the Panama Pacific half dollar. This issue is really quite rare in full uncirculated condition, a fact acknowledged by its $35.00 price as far back as 1955. Today it sells for hardly more than double this amount, which is a good indication of potential for future growth.

Another underpriced item is the Missouri with 2x4 added. This coin is three times as rare as the regular type, and has always been undervalued, even at the peak of the market. At today's price it is a steal.

One of the most depressed of all commemorative issues is the Fort Vancouver half dollar. It is at least as rare as the Missouri, and much more so if considered as a type coin. Yet, at the present time, it sells for only two thirds the price of the latter.

Compare the price of the regular Alabama issue for 1955 and then for 1970. Why has this coin, which was once so highly esteemed, sunken so low? The reason, in my opinion, is that the E.F.-A.U. specimens which doubtless comprise the majority of those available, are so often sold as uncirculated that collectors have come to believe it is a common issue. In full mint state, the Alabama is one of the rarest issues, and it is really worth a good deal more than it sells for today. An even more obvious discrepancy exists with regard to the 2*2 variety, which is almost twelve times as rare as the regular one. This coin actually belongs in a class with the Grant with a star.

Another good buy is the 1926 Sesquicentennial of American Independence issue. With a mintage of 141,120, it can hardly be called rare, but genuinely uncirculated specimens are few and far between, and are really worth a good deal more than their prices indicate.

The 1936 Arkansas-Robinson is likewise an undervalued coin. Its mintage would place it in the same category as the Wisconsin, Bridgeport and Elgin issues, and it is not more common than any of these.

Two coins which seem to me to be very underpriced are the Albany and Norfolk issues, and to only a slightly lesser degree, the New Rochelle. When we consider that the mintage of each of these three pieces is only about 50% higher than that of the hoarded Hudson and Spanish Trail coins, the prices of the former seem reasonable indeed.

Perhaps the most undervalued set of the whole series is the 1937 Boone. It is only slightly less rare than the 1935 with 1934 on the reverse, and has declined out of all proportion to the latter.

The Arkansas sets likewise offer a fertile field for the investor. With the sole exception of the 1939, I believe that every single set is a good buy at today's prices.

Aside from the particular issues mentioned above, I would suggest the commemorative series as a whole as one of the best long-term investments in numismatics. For one thing, as we approach our nation's bicentennial, more and more people will be growing interested in historical mementoes of all kinds. For another, the removal of silver from our coinage has made our silver and gold memorial coins appear just that much more attractive. And finally, the series offers a variety of handsome artistic types which really find no counterpart among the regular issues. With each new year, I would anticipate a growing number of new collectors, and a corresponding rise in the value of the series as a whole and its type coins in particular.

Finally, I would like to suggest to all collectors or would-be collectors of commemoratives that they get hold of a copy of Don

Taxay's *Illustrated History of U.S. Commemorative Coinage* which was published a few years ago. This book is an in-depth study of the artistic side of the series, and illustrates the various artists' sketches and models that led up to the adopted designs of each issue. It is a unique work and will prove immensely interesting to anyone who takes pleasure in the aesthetic side of our coinage.

AVERAGE RETAIL PRICES FOR COMMEMORATIVE HALF DOLLARS AS PER END OF YEAR

	Issue	Mintage	1955	1963	1964	1970
1892	Columbian Exposition	950,000	$ 2.00	$ 5.50	$ 6.50	$ 8.00
1893	Columbian Exposition	1,548,300	1.75	3.75	4.50	6.00
1915-S	Panama-Pacific Exposition	27,134	35.00	90.00	100.00	75.00
1918	Illinois Centennial	100,058	8.50	22.50	27.00	26.00
1920	Maine Centennial	50,028	7.50	27.50	30.00	25.00
1920	Pilgrim Tercentenary	152,000	3.00	9.50	11.00	21.50
1921	Pilgrim Tercentenary	20,053	6.50	19.00	22.50	54.00
1921	Missouri Centennial	15,400	53.50	117.50	147.50	120.00
1921	Missouri Centennial, 2X4	5,000	56.00	145.00	170.00	120.00
1921	Alabama Centennial	59,038	30.00	50.00	52.50	45.00
1921	Alabama Centennial, 2★2	5,000	34.00	75.00	75.00	65.00
1922	Grant Memorial	67,215	8.00	20.00	23.50	24.50
1922	Grant Memorial, with star	4,256	86.50	135.00	150.00	103.50
1923-S	Monroe Doctrine Centennial	274,077	6.25	15.00	16.50	15.35
1924	Huguenot-Walloon Tercentenary	142,000	8.00	25.00	25.00	25.00
1925	Lexington-Concord Sesquicentennial	160,013	4.25	13.00	14.00	17.50
1925	Stone Mountain Memorial	1,314,709	2.30	5.50	6.50	12.50
1925-S	California Diamond Jubilee	86,354	8.35	26.50	30.00	26.00
1925-S	Fort Vancouver Centennial	14,994	42.50	120.00	125.00	81.00
1926	Sesquicentennial of American Independence	141,120	6.25	16.00	18.00	16.50
1926	Oregon Trail Memorial	48,030	3.50	12.00	13.50	17.50
1926-S	Oregon Trail Memorial	86,354	3.50	12.00	13.50	17.50
1928	Oregon Trail Memorial	6,028	4.50	16.00	18.00	22.50
1933-D	Oregon Trail Memorial	5,008	7.00	16.00	19.00	33.50
1934-D	Oregon Trail Memorial	7,006	4.00	14.00	15.00	18.00

	Issue	Mintage	1955	1963	1964	1970
1936	Oregon Trail Memorial	10,006	3.65	12.00	13.50	17.50
1936-S	Oregon Trail Memorial	5,006	6.35	16.00	19.00	35.00
1937-D	Oregon Trail Memorial	12,008	3.65	11.75	13.50	17.50
1938	P-D-S set, Oregon Trail Memorial	6,005	13.25	33.50	40.00	50.00
1939	P-D-S set, Oregon Trail Memorial	3,004	53.50	115.00	125.00	130.00
1927	Vermont Sesquicentennial	28,142	14.50	50.00	52.50	37.00
1928	Hawaiian Sesquicentennial	10,008	98.50	495.00	525.00	450.00
1934	Maryland Tercentenary	25,015	10.75	50.00	55.00	34.50
1935	Hudson, N.Y., Sesquicentennial	10,008	62.50	280.00	325.00	230.00
1935-S	California-Pacific Exposition	70,132	5.00	20.00	20.00	17.50
1936-D	California-Pacific Exposition	30,092	6.25	23.00	23.00	—
1935	Old Spanish Trail	10,008	40.00	250.00	267.50	220.00
1936	Rhode Island Tercentenary	20,013	6.00	17.50	19.50	19.00
1936-D	Rhode Island Tercentenary	15,010	6.00	17.50	19.50	19.00
1936-S	Rhode Island Tercentenary	15,011	6.00	17.50	19.50	19.00
1936	Cleveland-Great Lakes Exposition	50,030	3.25	17.50	25.00	18.50
1936	Wisconsin Centennial	25,015	9.50	37.50	35.00	34.00
1936	Cincinnati Musical Center	5,005	21.50	130.00	150.00	120.00
1936-D	Cincinnati Musical Center	5,005	21.50	130.00	150.00	120.00
1936-S	Cincinnati Musical Center	5,006	21.50	130.00	150.00	120.00
1936	Long Island Tercentenary	81,773	3.50	13.50	18.00	17.00
1936	York County, Maine, Centennial	25,015	6.25	27.50	30.00	31.00
1936	Bridgeport, Conn., Centennial	25,015	7.00	30.00	32.50	40.50
1936	Lynchburg, Va., Sesquecentennial	20,013	10.00	47.50	52.50	37.50
1936	Albany, N.Y., 250th Anniversary	16,887	17.00	57.50	63.50	50.00
1936	Elgin, Illinois, Centennial	25,015	10.00	47.50	53.00	40.00
1936-S	San Francisco Oakland Bay Bridge	71,369	7.50	33.00	32.50	23.75

	Issue	Mintage	1955	1963	1964	1970
1936	Columbia, S.C., Sesquicentennial	9,007	12.50	33.50	37.00	43.00
1936-D	Columbia, S.C., Sesquicentennial	8,009	12.50	33.50	37.00	43.00
1936-S	Columbia, S.C., Sesquicentennial	8,007	12.50	33.50	37.00	43.00
1936	Arkansas Centennial-Robinson	25,265	8.50	30.00	30.00	26.00
1936	Delaware Tercentenary	25,015	10.00	47.50	55.00	43.50
1936	Battle of Gettysburg	26,928	10.00	47.50	52.50	42.50
1936	Norfolk, Virginia, Bicentennial	15,000	18.00	75.00	85.00	55.00
1937	Roanoke Island, N.C., 350th Anniversary	29,030	8.35	27.50	30.00	27.50
1937	Battle of Antietam, 75th Anniversary	18,028	27.50	95.00	105.00	82.50
1938	New Rochelle, N.Y., 250th Anniversary	15,266	20.00	80.00	85.00	62.00
1946	Iowa Centennial	100,057	7.50	17.50	22.00	24.00
1934	Texas Centennial	61,350	3.50	12.00	18.00	20.00
1935	P-D-S set, Texas Centennial	9,994	8.75	40.00	48.50	50.00
1936	Texas Centennial	8,911 }				
1936-D	Texas Centennial	9,039	9.00	42.50	48.50	50.00
1936-S	Texas Centennial	9,064 }				
1937	Texas Centennial	6,571 }				
1937-D	Texas Centennial	6,605	10.00	45.00	51.00	52.50
1937-S	Texas Centennial	6,637 }				
1938	Texas Centennial	3,780 }				
1938-D	Texas Centennial	3,775	39.00	95.00	135.00	110.00
1938-S	Texas Centennial	3,816 }				
1934	Daniel Boone Bicentennial	10,007	4.75	12.00	16.75	24.25
1935	Daniel Boone Bicentennial	10,010 }				
1935-D	Daniel Boone Bicentennial	5,005	14.25	40.00	40.00	47.00
1935-S	Daniel Boone Bicentennial	5,005 }				

	Issue	Mintage	1955	1963	1964	1970
1935	Daniel Boone with 1934 added	10,008				
1935-D	Daniel Boone with 1934 added	2,003	143.00	290.00	340.00	280.00
1935-S	Daniel Boone with 1934 added	2,004				
1936	Daniel Boone Bicentennial	12,012				
1936-D	Daniel Boone Bicentennial	5,005	14.50	40.00	40.00	47.00
1936-S	Daniel Boone Bicentennial	5,006				
1937	Daniel Boone Bicentennial	9,810				
1937-D	Daniel Boone Bicentennial	2,506	125.00	260.00	275.00	160.00
1937-S	Daniel Boone Bicentennial	2,506				
1938	P-D-S set, Daniel Boone Bicentennial	2,100	157.50	320.00	350.00	290.00
1935	Connecticut Tercentenary	25,018	21.50	43.50	55.00	49.00
1935	Arkansas Centennial	13,012	3.75	12.00	13.00	15.50
1935-D	Arkansas Centennial	5,505	5.00	14.00	14.75	17.50
1935-S	Arkansas Centennial	5,506	5.00	14.00	14.75	17.50
1936	P-D-S set, Arkansas Centennial	9,660	11.00	35.00	40.00	49.00
1937	P-D-S set, Arkansas Centennial	5,505	13.75	40.00	45.00	55.00
1938	P-D-S set, Arkansas Centennial	3,155	41.00	60.00	92.50	100.00
1939	P-D-S set, Arkansas Centennial	2,104	135.00	315.00	352.50	250.00
1946	Booker T. Washington Memorial	1,000,546	1.25	2.50	2.75	3.75
1946-D	Booker T. Washington	200,113	1.50	2.75	3.25	4.50
1946-S	Booker T. Washington	500,279	1.25	2.50	2.75	3.75
1947	P-D-S set, Booker T. Washington	100,000	6.00	11.00	15.50	17.50
1948	P-D-S set, Booker T. Washington	8,005	8.00	22.00	25.00	22.00
1949	P-D-S set, Booker T. Washington	6,004	9.35	35.00	42.50	35.00
1950	Booker T. Washington	6,004				
1950-D	Booker T. Washington	6,004	9.35	30.00	37.50	30.00
1950-S	Booker T. Washington	410,074				

Issue		Mintage	1955	1963	1964	1970
1951	Booker T. Washington	510,082				
1951-D	Booker T. Washington	7,004	9.35	26.00	31.00	31.00
1951-S	Booker T. Washington	7,004				
1951	Washington-Carver	110,018	1.00	1.50	2.25	3.00
1951-D	Washington-Carver	10,004	3.75	7.00	8.00	5.00
1951-S	Washington-Carver	10,004	3.75	7.00	8.00	5.00
1952	Washington-Carver	2,006,292				
1952-D	Washington-Carver	6,003	8.25	20.00	23.00	19.00
1952-S	Washington-Carver	6,003				
1953	Washington-Carver	8,003				
1953-D	Washington-Carver	8,003	8.25	25.00	26.00	20.00
1953-S	Washington-Carver	108,020				
1954	Washington-Carver	12,006				
1954-D	Washington-Carver	12,006	8.25	14.50	17.00	12.00
1954-S	Washington-Carver	122,024				
1893	Isabella Quarter Dollar	24,191	23.50	80.00	90.00	72.50
1900	Lafayette Silver Dollar	36,026	33.00	110.00	147.50	190.00
1903	Louisiana Purchase Gold Dollar (Jefferson)	17,500	25.00	95.00	100.00	77.50
1903	Louisiana Purchase Gold Dollar (McKinley)	17,500	28.00	95.00	100.00	77.50
1904	Lewis & Clark Gold Dollar	10,000	122.50	325.00	355.00	285.00
1905	Lewis & Clark Gold Dollar	10,000	110.00	315.00	347.50	275.00
1915-S	Panama Pacific Gold Dollar	25,000	16.50	82.50	75.00	70.00
1916	McKinley Memorial Gold Dollar	9,977	21.00	100.00	100.00	80.00
1917	McKinley Memorial Gold Dollar	10,004	24.50	157.50	157.50	127.50
1922	Grant Memorial Gold Dollar	5,000	70.00	335.00	355.00	237.50
1922	Grant Gold Dollar with star	5,016	57.50	307.50	330.00	232.50
1915-S	Panama Pacific Gold $2½	6,750	80.00	315.00	350.00	290.00
1926	Sesquicentennial of American Independence Gold $2½	46,019	17.00	70.00	63.50	65.00

Chapter 5
How to Profit with Regular Issue U.S. Coins

Those who write or speak of a general recession in American numismatics would be well-advised to look at the record. We have already examined the gains enjoyed by most of the older proof coins, and the present chapter will be devoted to an analysis of the regular issues.

The early 1960's was a period of unprecedented growth for the old coppers, that is the large cents and half cents. With regard to the cents, we need look for no further reason than Dr. William Sheldon's unique catalogue *Penny Whimsy*. This work has in a real sense set the standard by which all other die variety catalogues should and will be judged. On the one hand, its approach is scientific, working out die chronologies, exact rarities and a statistical method of pricing each of the items in each condition. On the other hand, it treats large cent collecting as a competitive sport, retaining the mood of the last century when collectors sometimes indulged themselves in a game they appropriately called "large cent whist." The result of Dr. Sheldon's books (for there have been two editions thus far) was not only a tremendous upsurge in the large cent market, but the publication of a special bulletin called *Penny-Wise*. There is probably no devotee of this series who does not subscribe to this informative periodical, and to date its circulation is around the 2,000 figure.

To understand just how bullish the large cent market was in the early 1960's, we need only consult the prices realized by the Helfenstein collection which was sold, during 1964, by Lester Merkin. Many of the winning bids were actually ten times the 1955 values, and that my friends is nothing to sneeze at. For the next few years, large cents continued to gain, after which the market as a whole levelled off. Smart collectors have no doubt been quietly taking advantage of this lull. There is little doubt that it will come to an end with the long-awaited publication of the third edition of Dr. Sheldon's book.

With regard to the 1816-57 cents, the only appreciable gains since 1964 have been in uncirculated coins which, on the average, have increased in value by about one third. Choice mint state specimens with original lustre still represent a good investment, and will doubtless get a good push whenever the early cents begin to move again.

The large cent boom of the early 1960's was in large measure paralleled by one in the half cents. For one thing, a great deal of new information on this companion series was made available for the first time through the very informative catalogues of the New Netherlands Coin Co. It was also announced that a new half cent catalogue, comparable to *Penny Whimsy,* would soon be published, and partly in anticipation of this event, collectors began to take a more avid interest in the varieties of this formerly neglected series. However, for a variety of reasons, the catalogue was never published and, eventually, when the large cent market began to level off, that of the half cents declined. As a result, auction sales over the last two or three years have furnished some very good bargains, especially with respect to higher priced material. One can only suppose that this trend will continue for the time being, and perhaps until a really definitive catalogue on the series is finally published.

Except for the very earliest issues of each denomination, and a few scattered examples among the later ones, investment potential seems always to be stronger for strictly uncirculated material. This is due to the fact that dealers, when purchasing a collection, and collectors who bid at auction, are generally willing to pay a proportionately higher price for such coins. The reader should not infer from this that circulated coins are a bad investment or that they cannot likewise return a profit to the holder, but simply that their movement is somewhat slower than mint state specimens. For this reason, the rest of this chapter in its general discussion and specific references will be devoted to the latter.

Of the earlier twentieth century coins, the Lincoln cents have undoubtedly suffered the most since 1964, and for the simple reason that they are tied by series continuity to the later issues which were sold as rolls. To give a few examples:

	1964	1970
1909 V.D.B.	$ 6.00	$ 4.00
1909-S V.D.B.	295.00	185.00
1909	7.50	3.75
1909-S	90.00	52.50
1910	8.00	6.00
1910-S	40.00	32.50
1911	9.00	6.00
1911-D	33.50	20.00
1911-S	55.00	35.00
1912	10.00	7.00
1912-D	45.00	35.00
1912-S	45.00	35.00
1913	10.00	9.00
1913-D	40.00	35.00
1913-S	42.50	28.00
1914	30.00	40.00
1914-D	625.00	450.00
1914-S	100.00	55.00

How long will this bearish situation last? In my own opinion, it will come to an end sometime within the next twenty-four months. For those who are reluctant to act now, I will give an extra piece of advice. The market of the early Lincoln cents is not only bound up with that of the later issues, but is actually a reflex of it. Consequently, the first indication that the early dates are again preparing to move will come as a sudden flurry of activity in the cent rolls. The time lag between the two will be sufficient so that if you are carefully watching the latter you will still be able to get in on the ground floor.

Also, please remember that certain dates, like the 1914-S, 1923-S and 1924-D, even when uncirculated, are almost never found bright. If you happen to locate one of the rare exceptions (of course, I mean uncleaned specimens!), and can pick them up at all reasonably, by all means do so. In a competitive situation they are quite liable to fetch a 50% premium.

There is much talk about the sluggishness of the flying eagle and Indian cent market, and for the last few years this has certainly been the case. However, a careful scrutiny of values between 1964 and 1970 is far less depressing than some of the talk I hear. The worst casualties have been for some of the higher priced material. For example, an uncirculated 1856 flying eagle cent, which had a peak price of about $3,000., can now be had for around $2,300. Again, the uncirculated 1909-S Indian cent has dropped some 50% from its 1964 price. Nevertheless, the remainder of the flying eagles and Indian heads have declined no more than 10-15%, which is hardly critical. In my judgment, the eagle and Indian cents will bounce back just as soon as the early Lincolns do so, and I have already given the reader a signal by which he can anticipate the latter event. All series have their cycles of popularity, and until the last few years the early small cents were in very great demand. There is no reason to doubt that this will again be the case, and soon.

Before moving on, I want to acquaint the reader with two exceptional blue chip investments in the Indian head series. These are the 1858 Indian head and 1859 with oak wreath and shield reverse. While generally considered as patterns, a quantity of both were struck for, and actually entered circulation. Accordingly, they have the same status as the 1856 flying eagle cent, and, what is more, they are considerably rarer. In the old Scott catalogues, these pieces were listed among the regular issues along with the 1856. Unaccountably, however, more recent catalogues have chosen to ignore them, and such is the power of the written word that, while the 1856 has realized prices in excess of $3,000., the transitional Indian heads have gone abegging. Now that the *Comprehensive Catalogue* has been published, and they are once more assigned their proper status, their values are bound to climb, both drastically and soon. In fact, they have already in the last six months increased some 50% in value, and this is only a faint hint of what they will be bringing two years hence. The wise investor will put away every single one of these he can lay his hands on.

The ephemeral series' of minor coins offer truly excellent opportunities for long-term investment. We shall begin with the two-cent pieces, of which a tabular listing of 1964 and 1970 unc. prices are given below.

	1964	1970
1864 small motto	$250.00	$200.00
1864 large motto	16.00	20.00
1865	16.00	20.00
1866	22.50	22.50
1867	23.00	25.00
1868	23.00	25.00
1869	24.00	27.50
1870	32.50	32.50
1871	55.00	37.50
1872	100.00	100.00

From the above, it can be seen that only the most modest gains have been registered by the commoner dates, while the rarer ones have generally suffered setbacks. From the standpoint of today's investor, this is perhaps just as well as it offers him an excellent opportunity to put away some undervalued items. To understand why I call these two-cent pieces "undervalued," you have only to compare their mintages with Indian cents for comparable years. For example:

$$1866 \text{ cent:}\quad 9,826,500$$
$$1866 \text{ two cents:}\quad 3,177,000$$

Now, despite the fact that the two-cent piece is over three times as rare, an uncirculated example sells for only about 25% the price of the cent. When you think about it, this is really quite extraordinary.

There are some who may doubt that the two-cent pieces are actually as rare as their mintages would suggest by comparison to the cents. This view, however, overlooks two facts, first, that the enormous quantity of common Indian cents lends to scarcer dates like the 1866 an undeserved aura of rarity, and, secondly, that the comparatively smaller demand for two-cent pieces makes them appear more common. In the years to come, when collectors will have turned to the latter series in far greater numbers, it may be expected to show a sudden and sharp increase in value.

This may be as good a place as any to remind collectors about allegedly "B.U." coins which are actually no more than cleaned specimens. That the practice of cleaning the older coins is becoming more and more widespread can be inferred from the simple fact that the number of available "B.U." specimens of nineteenth century coins has increased enormously over the last decade. Indeed, it is sometimes difficult to locate an advertisement for the older mint state coins in which they are not described as brilliant. Silver and nickel coins can often be artificially brightened without apparent harm, but the same cannot be said with regard to copper and bronze pieces. A B.U. two-cent piece, to deserve that description, must have a virgin surface. Such coins are a pale golden-brown in color, usually with some granular or edge toning. They are not any longer very common, nor are the genuine "red uncs.," which result from a slight but honest toning. Learn to discriminate between genuine B.U. pieces, which are always worth a good premium, and merely cleaned coins, which are not.

We come next to the nickel three-cent pieces, of which a partial tabular listing of 1964 and 1970 prices is given below.

	1964	1970
1865	$ 15.00	$15.00
1866	15.00	17.50
1867	15.00	17.50
1868	15.00	17.50
1869	16.00	19.50
1870	16.00	19.50
1871	22.50	23.50
1872	19.50	21.50
1873	18.50	21.00
1874	25.00	25.00
1875	40.00	29.50
1876	40.00	29.50
1881	17.00	20.00
1887	130.00	95.00
1889	25.00	29.50

Thus, the performance of the B.U. nickel three-cent pieces has been more or less the same as for the two-cent coins. I have already suggested that the latter would make a very good long-term investment, and this advice may be underlined several times over for the three-cent pieces. From 1869 on, there is not one single coin in this series with a mintage of even two million, and from 1879 on (excepting only the 1881) we are actually dealing in the thousands. It is truly amazing to see an uncirculated 1885 three cent piece, with a regular mintage of only 1,000 sell (in its infrequent appearances) for around $50.00. Smart investors could do no better than to buy up every single specimen of these rare dates and just stash them away.

Although advertisements abound for "B.U." nickel three-cent pieces, non-proofs in this series are virtually never found with any real brilliance. Moreover, they are frequently plagued by minute verdigris specks. If you can locate choice, well-struck specimens with a perfect surface (forget about the brilliance), they are worth a reasonable premium.

By contrast to the above, the silver three-cent pieces have registered gains of about 75% since 1964. Had I been writing this book seven years ago, I would have predicted just such a large increase as the series was then woefully depressed. Even as it stands, it offers room for growth, and I would anticipate an average annual increase of about 15% over the next five or so years.

Particular attention should be given to the uncirculated (non-proof) specimens of the 1863-87 coins, all of which are rarer than their proof counterparts, and, when catalogued properly, have been known to bring more than the former. The *Guide Book* prices for the 1863 and 1864 should be completely disregarded. As non-proofs, these dates have realized considerably higher prices as much as eight or nine years ago.

The shield nickels have on the whole about held their own since 1964, the only severe loss being in the case of the 1883/2 which was then newly discovered and had a market value of around $250.00. By 1970, the price of this particular item had dropped about 50%. Nevertheless, I think that in a large measure the continued popularity of the shield nickels has resulted from the many discoveries of interesting varieties, i.e. overdates, doubled dates, and in one instance a tripled date. The collector who, on his trips to dealers' shops, carries with him a sharp glass, will enjoy a great advantage over the average dealer who generally lacks the time, patience and/or knowledge to pinpoint the many rare varieties. This is especially true of the shield nickels because of the extreme minuteness of the date. I saw a good example of such "cherry picking," a couple months back when a friend of mine chanced upon a rare nickel overdate which had been catalogued by a dealer as an ordinary variety.

By contrast to the shield nickels, the Liberty head type has fared rather poorly, declining by about a third from its 1964 level. For the time being at least, I do not foresee much in the way of recovery, first, because the Barber Liberty head series is not particularly popular, and, secondly, because the rarity of the various issues simply does not warrant a much higher price.

The Buffalo nickels may be fairly said to have held their own, with some issues rising somewhat and others declining slightly. A few individual items may be recommended. The first is the 1913-S, type 1, which has fallen off by some 25%, and now sells for only a couple dollars more than the '13-D. In choice, well-struck up condition, it is an especially good buy at today's price.

Another underrated nickel is the 1917-P which, despite its mintage, is difficult to obtain in brilliant mint state. Choice, well-struck up specimens of all the branch-mint nickels from 1917-28 are also recommended when they can be purchased without a substantial premium. They are all exceptional, and worth from about 20 to 30% more than ordinary uncirculated specimens.

The seated Liberty dimes and half dimes seem to be pretty much as they were back in 1964, that is to say, very much undervalued. Imagine being able to purchase an uncirculated dime, more than a century old and with only a quarter of a million mintage for no more than $35.00! It's unthinkable, but there it is, a good indication of the opportunities still available in these two series.

For those of you who have recourse only to the more popular catalogues, I would call your attention to the following, first with regard to half dimes. The 1839-O, large O, 1844-O and 1864-S are all excessively rare in full uncirculated condition, and are worth far more than generally realized. The 1839-O is especially overlooked as the two mintmark varieties are not generally known and therefore distinguished.

The 1863-67 Philadelphia mint half dimes are all very rare as non-proofs, and their true value seems to be appreciated only by the *Comprehensive Catalogue*. If you can locate specimens priced according to other, more conservative catalogues, by all means buy them. But make certain that the coin in question is in fact a Philadelphia Mint issue. Frequently the S on the corresponding San Francisco half dimes is very weak, and on the numerous specimens that were used as buttons, may be practically obliterated. Even when dealing with uncirculated specimens, it pays to use a good magnifying glass.

The Liberty seated dimes are undervalued by comparison not only to most of the other series, but even to that of the corresponding half dimes. For example, an uncirculated 1861 dime, with a mintage of less than two million, can be purchased for around $30.00, while a comparable 1861 half dime, of which more than three million were struck, would cost, perhaps, a dollar more. And this is despite the unwritten rule that, all other things being equal, a higher denomination coin will always sell for somewhat more than a lower one.

In addition to recommending this series as a whole for long term investment, a number of individual blue chip items should be pointed out. These are all coins which are excessively rare in true mint condition, and which, in most catalogues, are very modestly priced. The list includes 1840 with drapery, 1841-O large O, either variety of 1842-O, 1845-O, both varieties of 1849-O, 1850 small O, and 1862-S. In addition, the *Comprehensive Catalogue* informs us that the 1843-O, 1858-S and 1859-S are all actually unknown in mint condition despite valuations given by other catalogues. There are a number of other dimes which are also extremely rare in full uncirculated state and which, together with a number of rare but generally unknown varieties, are listed in the *Comprehensive Catalogue*. You could do no better than to carefully study the sections of this work that are devoted to the seated Liberty coins. You will find a gold mine of information on various rarities which will enable you to be way ahead of the game. But don't wait, now that the facts are out, it is only a matter of time before they sink in and become part and parcel of normal pricing and bidding habits. Be a front runner and you will reap ample dividends in the coming years.

Neither the Barber nor the Mercury dimes have shown any particular increase in value since 1964, and no upswing, at least for the former of these, can now be foreseen. The Mercury heads are another story. Since the later dates exist in rolls, the series as a whole would inevitably advance as a reflex of renewed activity in the Roosevelt dime roll market. Keep an eye on the latter, especially during the next twenty-four months when, as I predict, it will again start to be bullish.

In the meantime, there are a few Mercuries which can be profitably obtained at today's prices. The first of these is the 1924-D. This coin is almost as rare by mintage as the '25-D, and is much less frequently offered in mint state. And yet, the usual price for the former is hardly more than a third that of the latter. This is a real blue chip item and cannot but eventually be recognized for what it is and valued accordingly.

Another undervalued dime in mint state is the 1931-P. Indeed, there are some who consider this issue actually rarer than the 1931-D or S, though it currently sells for only around 50% of the price of either one. I suspect that because of the absence of 1931-P nickels, the demand for dimes saved very few from circulation. In any case, it is an excellent investment.

Finally, if you can distinguish a truly mint state coin from a culled A.U., you would do well to buy any such examples you can find of the 1942/1 that are being offered at catalogue value. You will not have to wait very long for a profit, I assure you.

Whenever I look at the twenty-cent pieces, I am struck by the fact that the 1875 and 1876 Philadelphia mint coins, though almost fifty and one hundred times as rare (according to their mintages) as the 1875-S, sell for only 20-25% more. Admitting that the actual rarity ratio is somewhat less, these P-mint coins are nevertheless very much underrated. This seems to be a fairly recent occurrence, and due for the most part to the enormous demand for the '75-S as the commonest type coin. How long this trend will continue is anybody's guess. To reverse it, there will have to be a more widely awakened interest in collecting the series by date and mint. At the present time this does not seem to be too popular because of the unusually ephemeral nature of the series and the fact that, out of the mere seven issues, two are proofs and one (the 1876-CC) is extremely rare and high-priced. For all that, however, the series has done rather well for itself since 1964, most of the issues nearly doubling in value while the 1875-S almost tripled its price. I expect that this trend will continue for the time being.

By contrast to the seated Liberty dimes and half dimes, the quarters have shown a marked gain in the last six or seven years. To give a few examples:

	1964	1970
1847	$25.00	$65.00
1861	20.00	35.00
1871	17.50	55.00
1875	17.50	32.50

I anticipate continued gains of at least 10% per year for this series as a whole and somewhat larger increases for certain of the "sleeper" issues. The first of these is the 1843-O, small O. Most catalogues do not distinguish between small and large O varieties, and one must therefore turn to the *Comprehensive Catalogue* to learn that the small O is excessively rare in mint condition. The 1844-O, '47-O and '52-O are all examples of coins which, though modestly priced in the *Guide Book,* are likewise of the highest rarity uncirculated. In fact, most of the issues from 1840 through 1852 are very hard to come by in genuine Unc. condition, and may all be considered as excellent long-term investments. The same may be said of the S.F. mint quarters from 1855 to 1866. In fact, mint state specimens of the 1858-S, '59-S, and '60-S are actually unverified! Finally, the whole run of issues from 1880 through 1889 are very rare uncirculated, and worth a good deal more than the *Guide Book* would suggest.

Barber quarters have on the whole held their own since 1964, with sporadic issues both gaining and declining somewhat. Barber coins on the whole are not too popular today, and the quarters, like the dimes and nickels, do not seem to recommend themselves for investment.

While some of the later date Standing Liberty quarters have gained a bit since 1964, the series as a whole seems to have declined by about a third. This is rather curious since the series is an attractive one and most of the issues are genuinely scarce in mint condition. The present would therefore seem to be a reasonably good time for investment. But don't look for a quick profit. It may be a couple of years before the series picks up again, and even then, gains will be on the gradual side.

A large increase in the activity of bust type half dollars has been apparent for the past several years, and this is in large measure due to Al Overton's publication of an excellent die variety catalogue. However, even prior to this, there had been a growing recognition of the rarity of many early half dollar varieties and even certain dates in full uncirculated condition. Correctly valuing such issues has been something of a problem to the uninitiated due to the widespread practice of selling cleaned E.F.-A.U. coins as uncirculated, using comparatively low prices as a come-on. True uncs., especially for the earlier dates, are really quite difficult to come by, and they will be worth a good deal more than the "bargain prices" quoted for dubious pieces.

It is no exaggeration to say that full mint state bust type halves have actually tripled in value since 1964. Even then, I feel that this series will continue to gain by leaps and bounds for the next ten years. For one thing, it is the only other series of coins that can equal the large cents in consecutive mintages, quantity of varieties and general availability. For another, despite the publication of Mr. Overton's catalogue, there are still comparatively few collectors of the series. When we consider that there exist some two thousand dedicated large cent collectors, we have some idea of the long-range potential of the bust type halves. Of all the older U.S. series, it is the one with the greatest future ahead of it.

The large gains enjoyed by uncirculated Seated Liberty half dollars since 1964 (approximately 100%) is due to a number of factors. First of all, it has had the advantage of reflex action from the enormous gains registered by the bust halves. Secondly, it has benefitted from the generally increased interest of collectors in larger silver coins. And finally, there has been a growing realization of the rarity of almost all dates in truly pristine mint state. A few of these are to be specially recommended, namely the 1842 small date, 1848, and 1867-S. All of the 1879-91 half dollars continue to be undervalued because of the artificial ceiling imposed by the price of the proofs. A time may come, however, when, instead of being depressed by their commoner proof counterparts, the non-proofs will dramatically push up the price of the former.

As a series, the Seated Liberty halves still have plenty of room for advancement, and choice examples may be considered as a very good investment.

Despite a general disinterest in the Barber series', the half dollars have managed to register gains of from 10 to 25% since 1964. This is due primarily to the success of the earlier half dollars, and even should the trend persist, it does not seem a sufficient reason to recomend the Barbers for investment purposes.

In the Standing Liberty half dollars, the largest gains have been among the earlier and rarer issues which were previously underrated. At least one issue, the 1917-D (mintmark on obverse) still looks rather good to me. While it is not in the same class as the '17-S, it hardly deserves to be selling at only a third of the latter. Genuinely uncirculated pieces (as opposed to culls) continue to be a very good investment. I would not look to this series for any immediate upswing, but rather for a moderate steady growth over the years.

Silver dollars continue to be the most active coins in the numismatic market. The Seated Libertys have on the whole doubled in value since 1964, and will continue to show marked gains. Choice uncirculated specimens, with original lustre and a minimum of bag marks, are an especially good investment.

The Morgan and Peace dollar market is unique in many ways. For example, what other series of obsolete coins has ever been released in quantities of hundreds of thousands by the Treasury Department? In what other series has an issue [1904-O] dropped in value from $350.00 to $3.50? And what other series has ever been sold by the Government (as it is about to do with its remaining Carson City dollars) at the current numismatic rate?

Since our last event has yet to come, and since the others were already past by the end of 1964, they are not reflected in the tabular listings that follow. What the tables do show is a minor decline in most of the better Morgans and a somewhat sharper one in the Peace dollars. While this is, to some extent, due to the recent releases, it is largely a result of the general depression which, since 1964, has affected all of the more speculative series'. Nevertheless, there is a marked difference between these dollars and the various modern coins of other denominations. There are today, no more than a few issues of either Morgan or Peace dollars which can be truly said to be available in bag quantities. In fact, as more and more collectors continue to fill up the missing holes in their albums, even the supply of rolls is beginning to materially lessen. Yet, many of the earlier date dollars still sell for less than do quite recent Franklin halves of comparable mintage and which exist in incomparably greater quantities. To sum things up, the silver dollar market should be considered by investors as one of the best investments available at the present time. Ten years from now, we shall look back at the $3.50-$3.75 price for which many dollars are still obtainable as we now do to the pre-1955 prices for the various other series'.

With regard to specific issues, we may begin with a listing of those relatively few dates which were not found among the bags sold by the Government during the early 1960's. They are: 1889-S, 1892-S, 1893-P, 1894-P, S, 1895-P,O,S, 1896-O,S, 1897-O, 1899-S, 1900-S, 1901-S, 1902-S, 1903-S, 1904-S, 1921 (Peace), 1924-S, 1925-S, 1934-D, 1934-S, 1935-S.

When we examine the prices at which some of these items are currently selling for it is difficult not to get enthusiastic. For example, the 1889-S, with a lower mintage than the 1877 Indian head cent, sells in mint condition for only about $30.00. Moreover, this is about 43% less than it was bringing in 1964. Again, the 1893-P, with scarcely more than half the mintage of the '89-S, can now be bought for $50.00, that is, for substantially less than its 1964 price. And so on.

What of the other dates? New Orleans mint dollars from 1898-1904 have been released in sufficiently large quantities that we need not look to them for anything like immediate gains. Besides these, the 1883-87 P's, 1879-82 S's, and the 1883-85 O's seem to be available for fairly heavy trading. But for the rest, bags can seldom anymore be found. Rolls, of course, exist, but even these, as I have already explained, are growing fewer and fewer. To give but one example, while bags of the "common" 1878-S came out of the Treasury Department a decade ago, most dealers do not to-day have even a single coin in stock. And yet what does this issue retail for? A mere $4.50, or half the price of the common date Indian head cents which, incidentally, are also known to exist in rolls.

It will be seen that only a few dates among the Peace dollars were not included among the bags which came out of the Treasury Department. What is surprising is that three of these, the 1924-S, 1925-S and 1934-D, have declined by as much as the other dates which, relatively speaking, are now much more common. Accordingly, all of these may be recommended as very good investments.

It is no surprise that the Trade dollars are, for the most part, up 100% from 1964. Even as things stand the series is underpriced, and it is really very seldom that one sees genuinely uncirculated specimens offered for sale. With the predictable increase in silver dollar collecting, these rare coins can only increase in value and at today's prices they are an exceedingly sound investment. This is especially true of the commoner 1873-74 issues, most of which were melted down, and which still can be obtained, when available, for less than $100.00 each.

	1964	1971		1964	1971
1878 8F	$ 16.00	$ 14.50	1881-O	3.25	4.00
1878 7/8F	25.00	16.50	1881-S	2.00	4.00
1878 7F	5.00	4.50	1881-CC	67.00	65.00
1878-S	2.50	4.50	1882	3.00	4.00
1878-CC	12.50	15.00	1882-O	3.50	4.00
1879	2.75	4.50	1882-S	2.25	4.00
1879-O	7.50	6.50	1882-CC	23.00	35.00
1879-S	2.00	4.25	1883	2.65	4.00
1879-CC	180.00	185.00	1883-O	2.00	4.00
1880	3.75	4.50	1883-S	16.50	50.00
1880-O	4.50	6.00	1883-CC	22.75	27.50
1880-S	2.25	3.75	1884	3.25	5.00
1880-CC	55.00	57.00	1884-O	1.85	4.00
1881	4.25	4.00	1884-S	25.00	75.00

	1964	1971		1964	1971
1884-CC	31.50	37.50	1895-O	150.00	175.00
1885	2.00	4.00	1895-S	450.00	525.00
1885-O	2.00	4.00	1896	4.00	4.00
1885-S	14.00	12.50	1896-O	25.00	70.00
1885-CC	69.00	57.50	1896-S	165.00	165.00
1886	2.00	4.00	1897	12.50	6.00
1886-O	21.50	25.00	1897-O	15.00	40.00
1886-S	40.00	29.00	1897-S	12.50	10.00
1887	1.75	3.75	1898	6.00	4.50
1887-O	6.00	6.00	1898-O	4.50	4.50
1887-S	19.00	7.50	1898-S	32.50	20.00
1888	2.25	3.75	1899	33.50	20.00
1888-O	2.75	4.00	1899-O	2.50	4.00
1888-S	44.00	29.50	1899-S	52.00	27.50
1889	2.75	3.75	1900	3.00	4.50
1889-O	6.50	12.50	1900-O	2.00	4.00
1889-S	53.50	29.00	1900-S	25.00	29.00
1889-CC	800.00	875.00	1901	40.00	75.00
1890	6.00	4.50	1901-O	2.25	4.00
1890-O	5.50	10.00	1901-S	NA	40.00
1890-S	8.75	7.00	1902	8.00	7.00
1890-CC	23.00	25.00	1902-O	2.75	4.00
1891	25.00	7.00	1902-S	50.00	75.00
1891-O	10.00	12.50	1903	9.00	7.50
1891-S	16.25	8.00	1903-O	36.00	29.50
1891-CC	25.00	22.50	1903-S	225.00	350.00
1892	30.00	16.50	1904	20.00	17.50
1892-O	14.75	16.00	1904-O	3.50	4.50
1892-S	1000.00	1500.00	1904-S	NA	175.00
1892-CC	56.00	50.00	1921	2.00	3.75
1893	65.00	50.00	1921-D	7.00	5.00
1893-O	190.00	175.00	1921-S	8.50	5.00
1893-S	5000.00	4500.00	1921 Peace	40.00	40.00
1893-CC	150.00	185.00	1922	2.00	3.50
1894	275.00	165.00	1922-D	7.00	5.00
1894-O	30.00	50.00	1922-S	7.50	5.00
1894-S	56.00	40.00	1923	2.00	3.50

	1964	1971		1964	1971
1923-D	NA	10.00	1927-D	45.00	32.00
1923-S	7.25	6.00	1927-S	50.00	35.00
1924	5.65	4.50	1928	110.00	85.00
1924-S	42.50	30.00	1928-S	35.00	25.00
1925	3.00	5.00	1934	35.00	22.00
1925-S	27.50	15.00	1934-D	35.00	25.00
1926	20.00	8.50	1934-S	300.00	250.00
1926-D	21.50	10.00	1935	30.00	15.00
1926-S	11.00	6.50	1935-S	37.50	45.00
1927	41.00	25.00			

It is generally agreed that gold will one day be released from its fixed price in the Western world of $35.00 an ounce, and, perhaps, eventually even quadruple in value. But just when this is going to come about is still a big question mark, depending as it does so very largely on future U.S. policies regarding the dollar.

For the moment, and despite its apparent confusion, the situation seems to me to be comparatively stable. It is true that even if the U.S. secures a 10% devaluation of the dollar, this will provide only a short respite from its formidable balance of payments problem. On the other hand, no nation which owns a large stockpile of dollars would care to see their value too far undermined and thus lose a portion of its own money supply. Moreover, so long as the floating of the dollar is accompanied by widespread speculative buying and selling, it may be expected to maintain a tolerable if somewhat see-saw value. The only real threat, as I see it, would be if the U.S., pressed too stubbornly to settle its debts, were to unilaterally revalue the price of gold upwards or to announce a permanent cessation of gold payments. However, it is far more likely that even should it be so pressed, it would simply extend its "temporary suspension" ploy, leaving its allies with the indefinite opportunity to avoid a confrontation which would lead to international economic chaos. For at least the forseeable future, then, we need anticipate no real collapse of the dollar and only a creeping increase in the value of U.S. gold coins. Beware of any heady rumors like those which, a couple of years ago, briefly forced prices up sharply, only to let them down with equal suddenness.

PRICES FOR UNCIRCULATED GOLD TYPES AT END OF EACH YEAR

		1955	1964	1965	1966	1967	1968	1969	1971
$ 1	Type 1	$12.00	$ 40.00	$ 42.50	$ 45.00	$ 45.00	$ 47.00	$ 59.00	$ 65.00
$ 1	Type 2	20.00	275.00	300.00	250.00	325.00	375.00	470.00	500.00
$ 1	Type 3	12.00	45.00	50.00	52.50	52.50	62.00	70.00	70.00
$ 2½	Liberty	12.50	40.00	42.50	42.50	45.00	50.00	48.00	60.00
$ 2½	Indian	9.00	25.00	28.00	28.00	28.50	33.50	37.00	34.00
$ 3		42.50	237.50	285.00	295.00	275.00	275.00	310.00	320.00
$ 5	Liberty	13.50	21.00	21.50	26.00	26.50	34.00	43.00	32.50
$ 5	Indian	14.00	25.00	28.00	28.00	30.00	39.50	61.00	50.00
$10	Liberty	22.50	31.75	32.00	34.00	38.50	41.00	47.00	40.00
$10	Indian	24.50	36.00	42.50	45.00	50.00	63.00	71.50	60.00
$20	Liberty	40.00	53.00	53.00	51.00	59.00	67.50	70.00	70.00
$20	St. Gaud.	45.00	52.00	52.00	50.50	55.00	66.00	67.50	70.00

Chapter 6
How to Profit with Colonial and Early American Coins

Except for the present one, no generation of collectors has been so taken up with colonial coins as that of the 1860's. When we examine the prices of this early period, we should, of course, recall that the state copper coins had only dropped out of circulation a few years before and so were still readily available. In fact, we find them going at auction for anywhere from 2¢ in bulk to 10¢ a piece as individual items. However, with repect to the rarer material, the story is very different. During the 1860-65 years we see, for example, that collectors were already paying, for fine specimens, $25.00 for a New England shilling or Higley threepence, and $1.50 for a bar cent.

Much of this early enthusiasm was the result of continuing historical research, especially in the Boston area. This crystallized in 1875 in the publication of Sylvester Crosby's monumental *Early Coins of America*. Unfortunately, this great literary effort gave rise to no successors, and subsequent generations of collectors seem to have turned to other areas of numismatics.

As late as 1950, it was still possible to buy fine specimens of Connecticut or New Jersey cents for $2.00, a New England shilling or Higley threepence for $200.00 and a bar cent for $15.00. This is an average increase of only twenty times for the state coins and about ten times for the others, over a period of eighty-five years.

Then, quite suddenly, a spate of well-researched monographs re-awakened interest in the early issues. New historical background material together with listings of die varieties and revised rarity figures gave numismatists a systematic method of collecting which heretofore had been lacking in the series. Thus, within a decade, fine specimens of Connecticut and New Jersey cents had risen to about $7.00, a New England shilling or Higley threepence to $375.00, and a bar cent to $40.00. Using the 1860-65 prices as base values, we see that the state coins had now increased about seventy times, the New England shilling and Higley threepence fifteen times, the bar cent more than twenty-five times. That is to say, these coins had increased on the average more in ten years than they had for the preceding eight-five!

Research continued, new publications emerged and, by 1970, we had the following *Comprehensive Catalogue* values for the same coins in fine condition: Connecticut cents $12.50, New Jersey cents $25.00, New England shilling and Higley threepence $2,700.00 and Bar Cent $200.00. This is an appreciation over our base values of 125, 250, 108 and 133.3 times.

What is more, we find a disproportionate increase in the really rare items, the result not only of a growing expertise on the part of collectors, but also of a definite strain on the supply. The popular catalogues have occasionally been slow to catch up with the trends, as shown by the valuation, only a few years back, of $150.00 for a Standish Barry threepence, a coin which even then was selling for ten times that figure.

After its noticeably bullish stand for most of the last decade, the colonial coin market seems finally to have levelled off. Actually, this is about the worst we can expect from a field to which so many serious collectors are irrevocably committed. It is equivalent to the recessions which periodically hit the other series, and we may draw from it the same inference, namely that it offers a good time to buy.

Certainly the most desirable of all U.S. colonials is the 1652 New England shilling which is the first coin to have actually been struck in what later became the United States. Some fifty odd specimens are known today, a good many of which are impounded in museums. The value of these pieces has shot up dramatically in the last decade and now is about $2,700.-$5,500. This is already so healthy a price that it is difficult to anticipate any more real jumps in the foreseeable future. Nevertheless, the value of the coin may be expected to keep pace with that of the colonial market generally.

The same may be said for the willow tree shilling. Although slightly rarer than the NE type, it can hardly be said to enjoy the same historical status. At the present time, it is given a slight price edge, but this will probably be removed in the years to come.

Prices for the various oak and pine tree coins continue to be rather uneven in auction performance. The best investment in this area would seem to be type coins of superior condition, that is, in the extremely fine range. As yet, there do not seem to be enough collectors of die varieties to guarantee a really top bid for lesser material, even when it is quite rare.

The Lord Baltimore coins of Maryland seem to me to be a very good investment. Offerings are few and far between, and as the rarity of the series is really comparable to the New England and Willow Tree coins, prices could easily start soaring in the near future.

In the same class and even more undervalued is the Carolina elephant token. This is really an excellent coin to hang onto, if, that is, you are lucky enough to purchase one in the first place.

There is no question but that the whole series of 1783 Chalmers coins are very much depressed. When, for example, we consider that no more than about thirty specimens of the sixpence exist in any condition, the price of $550.00 for a very fine coin seems modest indeed. I predict that this particular series will show a very substantial increase in the near future.

Extremely fine and even choice very fine specimens of the state copper coinages will continue to rise in value, and at a greater rate than those in lesser condition.

One of the most undervalued of all early American issues is the 1790 Albany Church Penny. This is doubtless due to the fact that prior to the publication of the *Comprehensive Catalogue* it has never been listed in coin catalogues. And this despite the fact that these same catalogues list a number of English tokens which have no more than a fancied connection with the American series.

In all, there are probably no more than eight or nine Church pennies in existence. And yet, the specimen offered by Stacks in its recent sale of Massachusetts Historical Society material (and the first to be offered publicly in many a year) brought a mere $675.00. To give you an idea of just how great a bargain this is, one need only refer to the Standish Barry threepence, likewise a private issue of the same year, and of almost identical rarity. Today the Barry coin is valued from about $2,500. to $5,000.00! Even considering that it is a silver piece and rather more attractive than the Church Penny, the discrepancy is too obvious to avoid notice.

Another very great sleeper is, in my opinion, the 1796 Castorland half dollar, of which less than a dozen original specimens exist. In their infrequent appearances in public sale, these pieces bring no more than a high three-figure price. This is really very peculiar, especially when the Castorland is not only the largest private silver coin of the period, but quite attractive. I suspect that most collectors are not aware of the fact that these coins were actually intended for circulation, and that the majority did indeed circulate. Now that this has been clarified by the *Comprehensive Catalogue,* the issue should chalk up some substantial gains.

At around $2,000., the Myddelton halfpenny might also be considered undervalued. Only four or five specimens (I exclude the silver patterns) are known to collectors, and since the issue is proven by Mr. Taxay to have actually been struck for use in Kentucky, it is historically very important. Add to this the fact that it is a proof, and the most beautiful of all our early coins and you end up with quite an item. It could easily double in value over the next few years.

Chapter 7
How to Profit with Patterns

When, a little over a century ago, the Mint began to strike various additional patterns and cabinet coins for the benefit of numismatists, it seemed that the popularity of this series would soon exceed that of all others. Before long, however, the distribution of these pieces became unduly selective and collector interest gradually waned. It was not, in fact, until 1959, when the Whitman Company published the first edition of Dr. Judd's catalogue that the series once more began to attract attention. At the same time, a few prominent dealers such as Abe Kosoff, Q. David Bowers and Sol Kaplan started regularly featuring patterns in their advertisements, and two extraordinary collections, those of Lenox Lohr and Dr. Judd, were made available to collectors.

To appreciate just how far the pattern series has come since the first edition of Judd's catalogue, we have only to compare the valuations given in that work with the prices realized at Stacks' 1970 Di Bello sale. For example.

	Judd (1959)	Di Bello (1970)
J-362	$135.00	$ 775.00
J-416	75.00	1,000.00
J-1714	55.00	600.00
J-1717	70.00	490.00
J-1200	200.00	1,350.00
J-1205	300.00	2,100.00
J-1608	175.00	2,200.00
J-1315	50.00	375.00

In fairness I must point out that these are some of the more extreme increases, and that those of many other patterns over the same period are closer to about 300%. Why is it that certain items in this series have increased out of all proportion to the rest? In some instances, the answer is promotion, but even this doesn't tell the whole story since no pattern has ever been successfully promoted unless it offered a good peg for that purpose.

Take Judd number 416. This is one of a sub-series which is now known to collectors as transitional patterns, or patterns that are subsequently adopted and so differ from the regular issue only in their date. There was a time, and not too long ago, when these pieces were simply regarded as were any other patterns, and valued by the same general criteria. But then Q. David Bowers realized that these pieces could as appropriately fit into a collection of regular issue coins (especially proofs) as into one confined to patterns. For example, to someone who collected proof shield nickels, a series which begins in 1866, the 1865 transitional pattern would offer an interesting addition. As a result, transitional patterns soon became subject to a far greater demand and their prices shot up dramatically. The J-416 has, since 1959, increased in value nearly fourteen times!

Another group which has fared well is that of the more obvious mules, the two-headed pieces. J-362, the first item in our tabular figures, bears an Indian head on one side and a flying eagle on the other. Of course, such pieces aren't really patterns, but *pieces de caprice,* or special items that were made up for collectors who wanted to own something really unusual. Since many numismatists still have a taste for the exotic, and since these mules are always excessively rare, they can excite a really spirited bidding at auction.

Again, the silver patterns in general, like their counterparts in the other U.S. series, seem to have done better than average because of our present undue preoccupation with that metal.

Finally, a greater appreciation of the rarity of various patterns has assisted in their meteoric rise. For example, the Judd book lists certain patterns as rarity 7, which means from 4 to 12 specimens known. But it is obvious that a coin with an available population of only four specimens is very much more desirable than one of which three times that number are known. Gradually, as the statistics for the various issues have become more clearly defined, certain of the rarer R7s have become marked out as inherently more valuable. In this respect, the *Comprehensive Catalogue* is particularly useful as it not only corrects many of the faulty rarity ratings in the Judd book, but breaks down the R7 figures into low R7 (12 to 10 known), R7 (9 to 7 known) and high R7 (6 to 4 known).

In my judgment, the pattern series as a whole will continue to show marked gains, and is an excellent long-term investment. The greatest increases will doubtless be made in the more common items, which will be the first ones sought by the newer collectors entering the field. As a rule of thumb, I would say that any pattern, trial or experimental piece struck in its intended metal, or in the only available metal, which can be obtained for less than $200. is a good investment. In fact, many of these low-priced items are sufficiently rare that their entire supply might well be cornered by an enterprising individual.

For example, take the billon experimental pieces, J-111 and 112. These are currently priced by Judd at a mere $95.00 each. And yet, probably no more than two dozen specimens exist of either one, of which some are doubtless already permanently impounded in museum collections.

Then there is J-125, the only real pattern trime (apart from a few experimental patterns) and a very handsome little piece. Both Judd and Taxay (in the *Comprehensive Catalogue*) price it at a mere $150.00. But whereas Judd lists it as rarity 4 (76-200 pieces known), Taxay indicates that it is rarity 5 (31-75 pieces known). Very probably no more than about thirty-five or forty specimens are actually known, and as it is a single variety type it would seem to have plenty of room for price growth.

A couple of real sleepers are the 1850 and 1851 billon cents, J-119 and 127. Both are rarity 6 (13-30 pieces known), but their prices have been depressed by a variety of restrikes in different metals. J-119 and 127 are the only actual patterns for this inter-esting perforated issue, and the $75.-$85. price tag given by Judd and Taxay, though accurately reflecting the current market, is very, very conservative.

The several varieties of God Our Trust silver patterns for 1861 and 1862 seem somewhat undervalued as they currently sell for only about two thirds the price of the 1863 issues which are of equal rarity.

One of the most underpriced patterns in the whole series is J-221, the 1858 quarter dollar with regular obverse and pattern reverse by Paquet. Judd lists it at rarity 7, and prices the piece at $400.00. The half dollar of the same type he calls rarity 8 and prices at $2,750. Now if the quarter were a low-range R7, I could understand this enormous difference in the value of the two pieces. But Taxay defines it as the highest possible R7, with a mere four pieces known, or only one specimen less rare than the half dollar. This being the case, a more proper value for the former would really be about $2,000.00.

In the same class is the 1864 quarter with the Paquet design. This item is apparently of the same rarity as the 1858, and yet it is priced by Judd at a mere $135.00. Taxay has at least jumped the price to $400. to bring it in line with the 1858, but like the latter it is obviously worth about four times that figure.

A very much overlooked set is the 1864 silver quarter, half dollar and dollar with the motto In God We Trust. Judd, who prices these three pieces at $500., $600. and $750. respectively, indicates that they are rarity 7. Taxay more clearly defines them as high R7, and it is a·fact that not more than about five sets can be accounted for. When we consider that the rarity and transitional status of the set is not less than its 1865 counterpart, and that the latter sells for three and a half times as much, the moral is obvious.

There are also a couple of sleepers among the 1866 pattern nickels. For example, Judd prices J-467 and 481, which are rarity 7, the same as he does the least expensive R6 varieties. The descrepancy is most obvious with J-481 which Taxay indicates as high R7. This piece ought certainly to be worth double its current value.

Undoubtedly the most undervalued of all patterns is the 1867 nickel, J-565. Judd prices this at a lowly $175. despite the fact that only two specimens are known! This is only one tenth of his price for the equally rare J-632 nickel (which, moreover, is known only in copper), and less than he values some of the 1866 pattern nickels of which some two dozen specimens exist. It is unlikely that you will ever have the opportunity to bid on this great rarity, but in the event that you do I would suggest that you simply keep your hand up.

From where I sit, the two experimental dimes, J-714 and 716 look like rather nice buys. Judd lists these as rarity 6, but Taxay suggests that they are actually borderline R7. At $150.-$175., how can you go wrong?

Assuming that Dr. Judd's prices for the 1873 pattern trade dollars actually reflect sales records, there is something very peculiar about the bidding habits of collectors. For example, some of the commoner, rarity 5 pieces are priced at $400. and $450. while J-1300, with only three pieces known, is valued at $350.00. If you can purchase one of these, even at double that value, please consider it a good investment. As a matter of fact, the whole series of these pattern trade dollars seems somewhat undervalued and ought to be good items to put away for awhile.

The 1877 half dollars offer another fertile field. A number of them (when available, which is not often) can still be purchased at around $600., and since none are less than high rarity 7, this is quite reasonable.

Two extraordinarily good buys are the 1879 Morgan dimes, Judd 1586 and 1588, both of which are high rarity 7. Judd's prices of $175. and $200. respectively are, to say the least, conservative, especially when he prices the Barber dime pattern, J-1584 (which is a low R7), at $200.00. With a little luck you might be able to corner the market on the two Morgan issues for less than you would have to pay for a single 1856 flying eagle cent! The Morgan quarter and half dollar silver patterns for this year are also high R7, and I would offer the same comment regarding them. Judd prices the two halves at $360. and $300., while the lower R7 Barber half dollar is inexplicably valued at $1,000., or three times that price.

Before closing this chapter, I would like to call your attention to a whole group of "regular dies trials" listed by Judd which should be carefully considered for a long-term investment. Actually, most of these are not trial pieces at all, but proof coins struck in various metals for the benefit of collectors. It is not at all unusual to see these items going at auction for no more than a third the Judd price, because of their improper designation and the generally inferior status of patterns struck in off-metal. In the *Compre-*

hensive Catalogue they are for the first time listed correctly, in a section of their own following that of the regular proof coinage. Look over this section carefully and you will see that it offers a very interesting and rare series of coins at extremely conservative prices.

Chapter 8
How to Profit with the Great Rarities of U.S. Coinage

There are a number of United States coins which have always been regarded as the royalty of the series, and which, in their infrequent appearance at public auction, invariably generate a great deal of excitement. What is it that qualifies these particular items for their royal status? Rarity, of course, is essential, but it is obviously not the only consideration since there are a great many other excessively rare pieces which, by comparison, are virtual giveaways.

For example, there are the numerous unique trial pieces of various coins and patterns which often sell for no more than a few hundred dollars each. The explanation is that such pieces are still sought after by only a very limited number of collectors, and so do not enjoy the prestige of regular issues. To a lesser degree the same is true of patterns which, even after a decade of renewed appreciation, remain very much underpriced.

Again, there are the innumerable unique and nearly unique mint errors, some of which sell for as little as $20.00. The question is once more that of status, the value of these coins being determined more by the kind of error than by the date and mint of the issue involved. However, even the most precious mint errors do not stand a chance against our royal rarities, and this, incidentally, is one of the marked differences between the numismatic and philatelic markets.

Still another example is the die variety which, even when it is excessively rare, fetches a comparatively low price. Let me give you an example from my own personal experience.

A couple of years ago, I acquired, for a very nominal sum, a unique 1881/80 half eagle. At the time, this coin was virtually unknown, even to specialists in the gold series'. Out of curiosity, I placed it in a New York auction where, under something less than ideal conditions, it realized $150.00, the successful bidder being myself. At that price I would have been crazy not to buy the piece back, even though having to pay a consignor's commission. Besides, I knew it was about to be listed, with pedigree, in the *Comprehensive Catalogue,* which would immediately give it status in the eyes of thousands of collectors. It is a curious thing, but most collectors simply cannot get enthusiastic over a coin until after it has been "listed," and thus recognized by the general public. There are some who even wait until a hole has been made for it in the album of their choice! In any event, the 1881/80 was now "recognized," and to make things even better, a second specimen was discovered.

The layman will perhaps wonder why the fact that a coin has become only half as rare should make it more valuable. The reason is that unless a coin can build up its value through promotion (which is very difficult for an overdate), it must do so by successive appearances at auction. In that case, the existence of two or three specimens of an item is preferable to one simply because it can then be offered for sale more times and thus enjoy a greater possibility of advancement. It is very unusual for the owner of a newly discovered and still unique overdate to find a buyer who simply "must have the coin," and so is prepared to pay a really healthy price for it. One of the few exceptions which come to mind involved Al Overton, the Colorado dealer who, more than twenty years ago, discovered the first 1817/14 half dollar. At that time, Mr. Louis Eliasberg was still actively building his unique "complete" collection of regular issue U.S. coins, and decided that the new overdate was an indispensable acquisition. Thus, if I remember correctly, he paid something like 1,250.00 to buy it, a really fancy sum for those days.

But to return to the 1881/80 half eagle. I have said that the

coin was about to be listed in the *Comprehensive Catalogue,* and
I can now add that, as a result of that listing, I was able to sell it
a few months later for $500.00. The purchaser, Rarcoa Coin Co.
decided to offer the coin in its May auction. This raised an interesting situation since there were now thousands of collectors who, on
the basis of the *Comprehensive Catalogue* attribution, would have
thought I still owned the piece and had consigned it to the auction.
In other words, had I attended the auction and bid for the overdate,
the other prospective buyers would have quickly dropped out, assuming I was simply trying to run up the price. But though the
ambiguity of the situation would have proved very advantageous
to me as a buyer, I decided, in fairness to everybody, to stay away.
As a result, the coin now realized over $1,000.00. It was finally
coming into its own.

But the point I have wanted to make is that while the 1881/80
half eagle is excessively rare, its rarity is still ultimately that of a
variety. Had it instead been that of a date of mintmark, the coin
would have doubtless realized many, many times its current record
price.

There are also certain issues which, while they have only moderate rarity in the lower grades, are virtually unobtainable approach-
ing mint state. A good example of this is the 1799/98 cent, ordinary
specimens of which are always obtainable for a few hundred dollars. However, when, some years back, the first and only nearly
uncirculated specimen of this coin was introduced at a New Netherlands Coin Co. auction, it realized the then record price for a cent
of $10,500.00. This was and still remains a high price for a numis-
matic item, and yet, we cannot, for this reason, call the 1799/98
cent a "royal coin." On the contrary, we must reserve this term
for those pieces whose total population is sufficiently rare to guarantee in most instances a five-figure price.

We have so far defined our royal coin as a regular series date
and mint issue of extreme rarity. However, as we shall see, this
definition covers only a number of our candidates. The rest, indeed
the majority, have other claims to fame, and it is these we will
now examine.

Our first group consists of coins which would physically appear
to be a part of the regular series, but which modern research has

shown to have been made for presentation purposes, both officially and unofficially. For a time, when the historians were having a good deal of fun with these pieces, some people began to fear that their revelations would prove harmful to the market. Others, however, like Dave Bowers, realized that collectors enjoy nothing more than a good scandal, and are willing to pay dearly for anything that has come out of the mint under a cloud. The same opinion has been expressed by Don Taxay who writes that to condemn such pieces would be like spurning a Nero denarius because it is debased. Thus we see that one of the most important attributes of our royal coins is the story they tell, for this makes them valuable not only as coins, but as significant mementoes of Americana. For this reason also, our roster includes a number of items which are stories in themselves, though they have no place, even superficially, in a mere date and mint collection.

It is obvious that, in the case of five-figure priced coins, we are dealing with a rarified atmosphere in which only a small minority of collectors can breathe easily. Yet, there are few numismatists, of whatever means, who cannot get enthusiastic over such great treasures, and at least enjoy a running commentary on them and their market generally. So now, to the coins themselves.

The first of our "royal coins" is the 1776 silver dollar which the combined researches of Eric Newman and Don Taxay prove to have been struck under the supervision of the Continental Congress at a time when it was trying desperately to establish a mint. Brass specimens were also struck from the dies, in Mr. Taxay's opinion, as patterns for a contemplated penny coinage. Finally, there are the pewter pieces which seem to have been struck in early 1777, and presented to the various Congressmen to rekindle their interest in the mint project.

However, it is with the silver dollar that we are really concerned. Only three pieces are definitely known, all well circulated, and these are probably the survivors of a brief initial issue, struck, according to the evidence, around July, 1776. Since our founding fathers considered the Mint not only as an "emblem of sovereignty," but also as a means to support the Continental Congress, it seems probable that the emission of these first dollars was deliberately timed to coincide with the Declaration of Independence. Can any coin then have greater historical significance?

Of the three known specimens, those in the Johns Hopkins University Collection and that of Eric Newman will never be collectible. This leaves only the John Ford specimen, and a hypothetical fourth coin which has been rumored but not verified. In the absence of any public sales records for the last generation, it would of course be impossible to make more than an educated guess as to the current value of a 1776 silver dollar. However, were one placed on the market in 1976 (to create an ideal situation), and given the appropriate, widespread publicity it deserves, I would expect the coin to realize in excess of $100,000.00.

This seems as good a time as any to point out the unique place of the "royal coins" in any investor's portfolio. The matter may be summed up by saying that the prestige of these pieces places them in a category above and beyond mere numismatics, where they may comfortably sit alongside the other great historical treasures of our age. For example, a 1776 silver dollar is a virtual companion piece to an original draft of the Declaration of Independence. In varying degrees, most of the other coins we shall discuss have likewise some distinction or the other for which they may be sought in addition to their unusual rarity. These, then, are the "Rembrandts" of numismatics, and there appears to be no limit to the value which may eventually be assigned to them.

The second of our items is the celebrated Brasher's Doubloon, which, as a coin, has the unique distinction of serving as the theme of a motion picture. Excepting the unique Immune Columbia coin in the national collection, the 1787 Brasher pieces represent the only gold issue to have been struck in the United States prior to the establishment of the Mint. Nor is its romance lessened by the fact that Ephraim Brasher, its maker, was a well-known New York goldsmith and a friend and neighbor of President Washington. Some students have speculated that the doubloons, which are rather small and thick, were actually struck from dies intended to make the large copper cents used in those days. They point out that in the same year, Brasher had applied to the New York legislature for a franchise to coin such cents, and could well have submitted a doubloon or two as evidence of his work.

In any event, only three of the seven known doubloons remain today in collectors' hands. How much are they really worth? Once again, we are faced with a total lack of public sales records for anything like the recent past. However, my old friend Jack Friedberg, who owns the Coin and Currency Institute, values his specimen at well over $100,000., and I for one would not care to argue the point.

We come now to the 1792 dime (or disme), which Don Taxay has proven to be the first coin or pattern struck after the establishment of the Mint. Presumably the silver used to coin it was that deposited by President Washington, for whom some 1500 half dimes were struck shortly afterwards. The story of the 1792 dime is the story of our first U.S. Mint, which in turn is the first public building to have been erected by the Government. It is a story that must interest every student of Americana, and is the subject of one of Mr. Taxay's finest books.

Only two specimens of this piece are known to exist, one, with the date mutilated, in the Norweb collection and presumably non-collectible, and the other, superior specimen, ex Dr. Judd and now owned by my good friend, the California dealer and pattern specialist, Abe Kosoff. Mr. Kosoff has shown no urgency in disposing of the piece, knowing as he does that time can only enhance its reputation and value. I believe he has valued it at somewhere in the neighborhood of $50,000.00.

A second 1792 coin which seems worthy of inclusion is the copper cent commonly known as the "Birch cent." Though technically a pattern, this piece conforms to the weight prescribed by the 1792 Mint Act, and all specimens seem to have circulated in various degrees. There are three varieties (excluding the unique white metal trial piece), two with different lettered edges, and one, which is slightly less rare, having a plain edge.

According to a very old Mint tradition, the designer, Robert Birch, copied his profile head of Liberty from Trumbull's portrait of Martha Washington. This is a most interesting story, especially when we consider that his earlier pattern half dollar, which featured a bust of President Washington, had been rejected by Congress as "monarchical." Undaunted, Birch inserted the initials GWP (George Washington, President) into the legend of his first Liberty head cent, but it too was rejected. In the end, however, the artist seems to have gotten his revenge by placing an anonymous portrait of the first lady on the coinage.

It is unlikely that more than about eighteen specimens exist for all three varieties of the Birch cent, including those in museums and thus inaccessible to collectors. The *Comprehensive Catalogue* lists the plain edge variety at $13,500, the lettered edge ones at $15,000. each. As examples of the first United States cent, these are desirable coins indeed.

Our next item has frequently been called the "king of coins," and is one of the few, certainly, to have ever been the subject of a full-length book. It is likewise unique among our numismatic royalty in having been struck three decades later than its actual date. Thanks, primarily, to the efforts of Eric Newman, we now know that the first 1804 dollars were struck as specimen coins, intended and in part used for inclusion in gift sets for foreign dignitaries. We may recall that the silver dollar was discontinued by the Mint in 1804, and that all the pieces struck during that year were from leftover 1803 dies. However, the latter fact was quite forgotten by 1834-35, when the Mint was preparing to antedate some new specimen dollars with the last date of dollar coinage. And so a bonafide fantasy coin was created, although for an official purpose. In all, eight of these dollars seem to have been struck, of which, today, six (including a recently emerged museum specimen) are collectible.

But the 1804 dollar story does not end here, for, as Mr. Newman describes in his fascinating monograph, an additional seven pieces were struck in 1858, this time under more controversial circumstances. As a matter of fact, the issue seems to have been the private project of the son of one of the Mint's principal officers. However, the young man apparently lacked the means to letter the edges, which fact easily identified the coins for what they were. After a minor scandal, the Mint announced that the coins (some of which were sold and then retrieved) had been destroyed, but as it turned out they were merely hidden away. Subsequently, Mint Director Henry Linderman surreptitiously brought them out of hiding and lettered their edges. Since Linderman himself was an avid coin collector, it is not surprising that one specimen should have found its way into his own cabinet. All but one of the remaining restrikes were then disposed of, accompanied in some cases by curious official testimonies of their 1804 origin. At the present time, four of these pieces are still collectible.

Because of the comparatively "large" number of available specimens, the 1804 dollar has enjoyed an advantage given to few of our other "royal coins." In the last twenty years, for example, 1804 dollars have been featured in no less than seven sales, invariably setting new price records.

The following list of 1804 dollar auction records, ranging as they do over more than a century, will I think interest the reader. The specimens are differentiated according to the two (1834-35 and 1858) issues.

1867 (I)	$ 750.00	1941 (I)	$ 4,250.00
1883 (II)	740.00	1946 (II)	2,875.00
1885 (I)	1,000.00	1946 (I)	10,500.00
1888 (II)	660.00	1950 (II)	3,250.00
1890 (I)	570.00	1950 (II)	3,400.00
1904 (I)	1,100.00	1954 (II)	8,000.00
1907 (I)	3,600.00	1960 (II)	28,000.00
1913 (II)	340.00	1961 (II)	29,000.00
1918 (I)	2,500.00	1963 (II)	36,000.00
1922 (II)	840.00	1970 (I)	77,500.00

One of the interesting facts revealed by the above list is that collectors, at least in the old days, distinguished rather sharply between the status of type I and type II coins. Whether this descrimination continued after 1950 it is impossible to say due to the sudden disappearance of the type I's. Similarly, we cannot know whether the fantastic 1970 price for a type I reflects an appreciation of its particular status or merely an extraordinarily avid siege of bidding. A curious sidelight is the fact that the first 1804 dollar ever offered at auction, one hundred and four years ago, turns out to be the same coin that brought the record $77,500. in the recent Stacks sale. Even more strange is the history of this coin, which after being bequeathed by the famous numismatist William Appleton to the Massachusetts Historical Society, has finally returned to the collecting market.

Since we are already on the subject of clandestine coinages, we may appropriately exhaust our list before moving on to other of our royal coins. Proceeding chronologically, we come next to the fabulous 1866 no motto silver proofs (quarter, half dollar and dollar) which, by any standard, are rarities *par excellence*. Mr. Woodin, an ex Secretary of the Treasury, whose collection of patterns formed the basis of the Adams book, liked to call these pieces transitional patterns. The same attribution was later adopted by the Judd work on essays. However, a number of years ago, the pattern authority Dave Bowers pointed out that this attribution would erroneously imply that the pieces in question were struck prior to the adoption of a new design when, in fact, the opposite is true.

The question then arose of whether the 1866 no motto silver pieces might not be considered as regular proofs, struck right before the changeover. However, this too seemed unlikely since the Mint's anual report specifically stated that the motto appeared on all of the year's coinage. Of course, we know that a good many 1866 no-motto coins were actually struck and circulated by the San Francisco Mint, but this seems to have been due simply to the time lag in getting new dies to the West Coast. Since no such problem existed for the mother mint in Philadelphia, the obvious solution is that the no-motto proofs struck by the latter were simply a concession to one of the more influential collectors. The argument is further strengthened by the fact that this was a common practice of the period.

Mr. Bowers, who is really the author of the above view, has further clarified it by drawing up a list of the various pieces which unofficially perpetuate a series that has been officially discontinued. These pieces are now known as "simulated series coins," and, as we shall see, they are well represented in our royalty.

Both the 1866 no motto quarter and half dollar are unique, while two of the silver dollars are known to exist. Unfortunately, the present whereabouts of three of the four coins is very uncertain since they were among the items stolen from the great Dupont collection. It would certainly be a pity if these treasures were irrevocably lost to the numismatic community.

The last public appearance of the quarter and half dollar was at the Hydeman sale conducted in 1961 by Abe Kosoff. At that time the quarter realized a price of $24,500.00 while the half dollar brought $15,500.00. Today, they would doubtless be worth at least double that amount.

The highest price ever realized for the dollar was at the Wolfson sale held in 1963 by Stacks of New York City. The coin there realized $18,000.00.

The 1884 and '85 trade dollars enjoy the distinction of being the only coins whose striking was ever officially denied during the same year. They seem to have been struck for the most part for William Idler, a great favorite of the Mint officials and a man very good at keeping secrets. However, even the most closely guarded secrets sometimes have a way of leaking out, and when, in 1884, rumors to the effect that the Mint was still "quietly manufacturing" trade dollars reached the ears of other Philadelphia collectors, they naturally protested. Repeated denials were issued by the Mint, and based on these *Numisma* magazine even offered a reward for anyone who would produce such a coin. Of course, no one came forward, and it was not until the marketing of the Idler collection in 1907 that the existence of these pieces was finally confirmed.

It is believed that ten trade dollars exist for 1884 and five for 1885 together with a unique copper strike of the former date. The highest price so far realized for an 1884 is the $8,750.00 paid for the Wolfson coin. Disappointingly, a specimen brought only $6,300. in 1969. The record for an 1885 Trade dollar is the $11,000. realized by the Ewalt coin in 1965.

When we consider that both issues are comparable in status to the 1913 Liberty head nickel, and that the 1885 is equally rare, the above prices are obviously conservative. Unfortunately, neither of the trades have ever been the subject of a million dollars worth of advertising and promotion which the late Max Mehl is said to have spent on behalf of the "king of nickels." So there they are, royalty to be sure, but as yet woefully undervalued, and two of the best buys I can think of for the numismatist who can afford them.

And so we come to the 1913 Liberty head nickel, which is probably the most famous of all numismatic rarities. Don Taxay has shown us that all five of the known pieces were originally owned by one Samuel Brown who was storekeeper at the Mint when the coins were struck and so presumably can be held responsible for their manufacture. Like the 1884-85 Trade Dollars, the 1913

Liberty nickels were made surreptitiously and their very existence remained wholly unknown until 1919 when Brown placed an ad in *The Numismatist* offering to pay $500.00 for any specimens offered to him. Since he himself owned the only pieces made, it is obvious that he was simply trying to build up their value. In the following year, he offered the set of five for sale through a Philadelphia dealer, and they subsequently wound up in the famous Colonel Green collection. They were later dispersed, with two of the five at one time belonging to King Farouk.

The way in which the 1913 Liberty head nickel became so widely known is also an interesting story, and it involves the late B. Max Mehl who was one of the most successful coin dealers of all time. Mehl claimed to have spent over a million dollars in advertising to get people to send him the various old coins they had lying around the house. As a bait, he would offer to pay $50.00 for a 1913 Liberty head nickel. Of course, no one ever found a genuine piece, but the very thought that they might be able to get $50.00 for a mere five-cent coin generally induced them to send to the Texas dealer whatever they had. As a result, people everywhere began to reexamine the contents of those old boxes and jars that their parents and grandparents had set aside, and numerous rare coins which otherwise might have been eventually turned in for redemption were saved for future generations of collectors. And, of course, the 1913 Liberty head nickel became a virtual byword for a numismatic treasure.

In recent years, there have been only two opportunities for collectors to bid for these celebrated nickels. The first occured in 1961, when the Hydeman specimen was placed on the block, accompanied, however, by a $50,000.00 reserve. Bidding was spirited, but, in the end, it stopped slightly below the reserve, leaving the coin to go back to its owner. In 1967, a specimen was finally sold at the A.N.A. convention sale which was conducted by the Paramount Coin Corp. Aubrey Bebee, the well-known Nebraska dealer, was the successful bidder, paying a price of $46,000.00.

In a somewhat different category are our next two items, the 1838-O half dollar and 1894-S dime. Technically, both coins belong to that very select group of early branch mint proofs, but above and beyond this, each represents the only coinage struck for its particular date and mint. Consequently, they are eagerly sought after by all those who would possess as complete as possible a set of "regular issues."

Almost all of the branch mint proofs seem to have been struck as presentation pieces to commemorate an important occasion. The 1838-O half dollar was issued to celebrate the opening of the New Orleans mint in that year. Although twenty pieces are known to have been struck, no more than a dozen can be accounted for today. The highest price ever paid for one is the $14,000.00 realized at the Stacks Jay sale in 1967.

The 1894-S dime is somewhat more mysterious in its origin, but may have been made to commemorate the fortieth anniversary of the San Francisco mint. Of the twenty-four pieces struck, only about a third of that number survive today. The rest were apparently circulated and eventually turned in for redemption. Interestingly, a single well worn specimen exists, and was recently purchased by one of my friends on the staff of *Coin World*.

The record price for an 1894-S dime is still the $13,000.00 paid in 1961 for the Hydeman coin. I would not be surprised however, if a considerably higher amount were realized by this coin in the near future.

Except for the 1776 silver dollar, I would unhesitatingly call our next item the most important single coin in the entire field of American numismatics. Like the former piece, it was struck as an "emblem of sovereignty," in this case by the rebel Confederate government which hoped to demonstrate in unmistakeable terms its independence from the Union. Again, the Confederate venture, like that of the Continental Congress, failed to materialize due to an inability to obtain the necessary bullion.

The existence of the Confederate half dollar remained unguessed throughout the Civil War, coming to light only in 1879 when Dr. B.F. Taylor, the C.S.A. chief coiner consigned the original reverse die together with one of the four patterns struck to the coin dealer Ebenezer Mason. Both items were then sold to Scott & Co. of New York, which proceeded to restrike some 500 pieces.

The Taylor specimen was subsequently bequeathed to the American Numismatic Society in whose collection it today resides. If the history of the other three specimens were fully known, it would doubtless make very interesting reading. For strange to say all somehow got into circulation, including that presented to and originally owned by Jefferson Davis! It is difficult to imagine that such treasured mementoes would be so little esteemed when the cause for which they were struck entailed the loss of innumerable lives. Equally strange is the fact that after once entering circulation, all three should have eventually been culled out and again found their way back into collectors' hands. But there it is. Today all four original Confederate half dollars are accounted for, two of the circulated pieces having come to light only in the last decade.

The Eric Newman specimen is not expected ever to be accessible to collectors, leaving us with the two coins that are owned, respectively, by John Ford and Lester Merkin. Since no public sale record can be cited since the sale of the Taylor-Scott coin in 1879 for $1,000.00, any present estimate can only be conjectural. However, when we consider that no 1804 dollar managed to exceed this price until the present century, it would be a conservative appraiser who today would value a Confederate half dollar at less than six figures.

Among the various private gold coins issued during the California gold rush there are really a considerable number which we might call numismatic royalty. For example, a Kellogg & Co. $50.00 gold piece, of which some thirteen specimens are known, has a record sales price of $22,500.00. This makes me wonder, in all conscience, just what the unique U.S. Assay Office $200.00 gold piece owned by John Ford would bring if and when it ever came on the market!

Among the greatest rarities of the Colorado gold issues are the John Parsons & Co. and J.J. Conway & Co. issues, all of which, with one exception, have individual populations of no more than a half dozen pieces. No coin of these companies can expect to get through an auction at less than $10,000., and most could easily double that figure. In the same class we must place the Mormon $20.00 coin and the Oregon Exchange $10.00 gold piece. And yet, these are only the private gold coins we may reasonably appraise. There remain a large number of issues which are unique or nearly so, and for which, therefore, any price is possible should they ever come under the hammer.

From all this it should be clear that the status of these gold rush issues is really quite on a par with that of the Mint's own coins. And in time, it might even be greater. For with the tremendous renewal of interest by affluent collectors and museums for artifacts of the old West, there is really no limit to the possibilities inherent in "Pioneer gold" coins.

There remain a number of regular U.S. coins which, solely on the strength of their individual rarity, have made a place for themselves among our royalty.

It may be argued that the first of these, the 1849 $20.00 gold piece, should not be listed at all since it is unique and will remain forever in the national collection. This, of course, is a widespread belief, but there is a good chance that it may be incorrect, as the *Comprehensive Catalogue* also suggests. First of all, we know that two pieces were actually struck, the second having been sent to Secretary of the Treasury Meredith. Secondly, Walter Breen chanced upon a photograph of an 1849 double eagle among the effects of the late S.K. Nagy, and he is convinced that the coin shown was neither the Mint specimen nor the gilt copper piece last seen at the Woodside sale of 1892. Since Nagy was related to William Idler, one of the all-time favorites of the Mint, and since his collection contained many unique and otherwise unknown patterns, the presence of the photograph could be significant. Admittedly the coin itself was not among Nagy's collection, but that in itself does not tell us much. Since we know from experience that even an 1804 dollar can remain in hiding for more than a century, why could not an 1849 double eagle?

Should the piece ever turn up and be offered for sale, it is safe to say that it would shatter all records by a sizeable margin. Let us wait and see.

After the hypothetical 1849, the most prized double eagle is the 1907 issue with extra high relief. Like the former, this piece is a pattern representing an unsuccessful first attempt to make dies for a new design. There is a curious discrepancy between the number of specimens supposedly struck of this piece and that which can today be accounted for. According to an early statement by the Mint, twenty-two extra high relief double eagles were struck before the experiment was discontinued as unsatisfactory. Moreover, the late Farran Zerbe is said to have once stated privately that the then

Mint Director and Chief Engraver caused additional pieces to be struck under unofficial circumstances. It is doubtful, however, if more than thirteen or fourteen of these coins can today be located. Certainly their appearances at auction are few and far between, and it is difficult to complain about the $32,500.00 price realized nearly a decade ago.

In the same class as the above, and just a few pieces rarer, is the 1927-D double eagle. To date, the $32,000.00 brought by a specimen in 1969 is the highest ever realized by a regular issue coin of that denomination.

We will now skip down to the half eagles where, among a cluster of rarities, we find a couple which are worth special mention. The foremost of these is, of course, the 1822, of which only three are known, two being in the national collection. It is a great pity that the Smithsonian Institution should now possess two of these pieces, and we can only hope that one of them will some day be traded or sold off and so again become available to collectors. If not, there is only the Eliasberg coin, whose ultimate fate remains unknown. There is little doubt that if it or either of the other two pieces were marketed today, they would realize in the neighborhood of $75,000.00.

If we add together the known specimens of both varieties of 1829 half eagles, we are hard put to account for a dozen coins. Moreover, as the issue is generally broken down by collectors into large and small date coins, the rarity of each becomes doubled. Even so, however, the $21,500.00 price realized by the latter in the 1963 Florida sale seems to me rather exceptional. In any case, it will be interesting to compare this figure with that realized by the equally rare small eagle 1798 and 12 star 1832 if and when either of these pieces come onto the market.

A half eagle that would really bring a fancy price on today's market is the 1841-O. With an original mintage of a mere fifty coins, only two survivors and one collectible specimen (whereabouts unknown) this is certainly one of the highlights of the gold series. Another, of course, is the 1854-S, of which only three pieces are known, and two definitely collectible. That the specimen in the great Wolfson sale brought only $16,500.00 seems rather surprising, especially when we consider the price realized during the same year by an 1829 half eagle.

Among the three dollar gold pieces, the 1870-S stands unrivalled. Whether the one known specimen is that supposedly placed in the cornerstone of the second San Francisco Mint, or a second, unrecorded specimen, we shall probably never know. In either case, the Eliasberg coin has no stand-in and, except for the unconfirmed second specimen of the 1849 double eagle, must be considered as the single most valuable regular issue U.S. coin. To get some idea of what the 1870-S might bring under the hammer, one has only to consider the 1875 three dollar piece which, as the runner up of the series with about thirty known, realized $25,000.00 at the 1968 Miles sale.

The last gold coin we need mention is the 1841 quarter eagle, of which a half dozen specimens are collectible and two other permanently impounded in museums. As a middle range R7 issue, this coin has done all right for itself, chalking up an impressive $18,000.00 price in the 1968 Shuford sale held by Abe Kosoff.

There are perhaps only three of the regular silver issues that really qualify as royal coins. The first is the 1870-S dollar of which six or seven specimens are known. One of these, the Wolfson coin, realized $12,000.00 in 1963 and then chalked up a more than 50% gain by bringing $19,000.00 in the Miles sale.

Considering that there exist today no more than eight original 1827 quarters, it seems astounding that four of these were actually paid out at face value in the year of their issue. Today some six specimens remain in collectors' hands, with the record price of $16,000.

Of about equal rarity with the last, and the final of our royal coins is the 1876-CC twenty-cent piece. Coincidentally, it also has a record in the Miles price of $16,000.00.

For those who are really interested in obtaining some of the coins mentioned in this chapter, I have one very important rule to offer, namely that no coin, however rare and desirable, can achieve its full potential in a vacuum. In other words, if you intend to auction off a collection which is comparatively small and of mostly mediocre quality, it will not pay to include, say, an 1884 Trade Dollar, even if you happen to own one. The reason is that you simply won't be able to draw as many of the potential customers for the coin, or generate the same amount of enthusiasm among those who do attend. To get the most for your rarity (at least at auction), it should always be accompanied by as many other rarities and fine coins as possible. Moreover, they should be basically coins of the same kind. If, for example, you own an outstanding set of large cents, there is little to be gained by tacking on a few other choice silver or gold coins. Whenever you are in New York City, stop off at the American Numismatic Society and spend some time examining the prices realized in the various sales. You will find that even in the case of our royal coins, a proper environment is essential.

Chapter 9
How to Profit with Foreign and Ancient Coins, and Primitive Money

Considering the close connection that exists between Canadian and American numismatics, it is not surprising that the former has to some extent paralleled the trends of the latter. In the 1960's, for example, heavy speculation in modern U.S. coins inevitably poured over into the Canadian series', inducing numerous Canadian collectors to likewise become part or full time dealers. As with the U.S. issues, there was an initial sharp upswing followed by a rather precipitous decline.

Today, the situation is largely normalized. The speculators have either departed or grown more subdued, and many of the more serious collectors who had left the hobby are returning to the ranks. Moreover, if the modern Canadian issues remain depressed, the older, choicer material has mostly held its own or gained since 1964. The only real exception is the large cent series, which seems on the average to have dropped by about a third, and therefore offers a very attractive incentive for investment. For example, a "common date" cent like the 1901, with an entire mintage of scarcely more than four million, can still be acquired in mint state for a mere $10.00.

There are also many opportunities among the silver five-cent pieces. The 1887 and 1894 coins, with mintages of only a half million each (the second lowest in the series), today sell for about

$90. and $50. respectively. Some of the other dates, like the 1882-H, which have dropped by about 25% since 1964, should also be considered. In the early dime, quarter and half dollar series', where strictly uncirculated specimens are almost invariably difficult to obtain, things are even more hopeful. Don't look for short-term profits, but rest assured that in the years to come the many new collectors who will compete for these coins will inevitably force a dramatic rise in their value.

But Canadian coins are only one small segment of our global numismatc picture, and from the investment view not necessarily even the best. In fact, there are many other areas of foreign coins which, by comparison, offer almost virgin opportunities.

As a whole, foreign coin collecting did not attain much popularity in this country until the last decade or so. It was then, due to the high prices already realized by U.S. material, that many collectors began to look around for various other series' which could be more modestly acquired. At the same time, many persons were drawn to world coins because of the wider educational perspective they offered.

As soon as this happened, the next step was inevitable, namely the breaking down of each foreign series into different dates, mints and varieties. Heretofore, few collectors had bothered about any but type coins, but once started, the new trend gained popularity everywhere. There is little doubt that within a decade or so, the coinage of virtually every nation on earth will be catalogued and priced according to the rarity of its individual issues.

Consequently, the present time would seem to offer an ideal one for investing in the foreign field. Today's market, though active, is still not that much higher than it was six or seven years ago. In a sense, it might be compared with the U.S. coin market prior to 1955. And who wouldn't be glad to purchase material at those early prices?

Those who know me as almost strictly a dealer in U.S. coins and currency may be surprised at the inclusion of this chapter and its recommendations. But it is only fair to the reader that he be made acquainted with *all* the investment opportunities of numismatics and not merely with those from which I personally derive an income. And if my treatment of the foreign field is by necessity somewhat generalized, I will try to make up for it by giving the reader one very good tip—namely that he subscribe to (and try to read back issues of) the auction catalogues produced by my old friend, N.Y. dealer Hans Schulman. I say this because Mr. Schulman is not only a leading dealer in general foreign coins and medals, but also in ancient coins, artifacts and primitive money. To the budding collector especially, such a wide exposure will prove very helpful in crystalizing his fields of interest. It will enable him also to better understand and appreciate the vast possibilities inherent in coin collecting. For example, few persons unacquainted with the extent and scope of ancient coins would ever guess that there are more than 100,000 different specimens in the cabinet of the American Numismatic Society. Of course, no individual can hope to equal a record like this, nor, indeed, is it at all necessary in order to enjoy these antique pieces. Ancient coins are generally collected by city, and within the city by type and sometimes denomination. From the time of Alexander the Great, these beautiful pieces can also be collected by ruler, and there is no more impressive display than, say, a series of choice tetradrachms showing the various kings of Macedon, Syria and Parthia.

The earlier Greek coins are interesting for another reason, namely their depiction of the various gods, religious cults and votive symbols of all kinds. It is no exaggeration to say that a book could be written on the various emblems found on any one Greek coin.

If the Roman imperial series is somewhat less significant in this respect, it more than compensates by its rich historical and political allusions. Temples, bridges, harbors, marching soldiers, prisoners of war—these are but a few of the innumerable commemorative devices that oppose the emperor's bust.

Ancient coins also lend themselves to various specialized collections, as for example Biblical coins. Imagine being able to own a genuine "tribute penny," a Pontius Pilate "widow's mite," and a representative of the "thirty pieces of silver," all for only about $300.00. Again, one can collect topically, acquiring the different depictions of boats, vehicles, animals, musical instruments and so forth. The possibilities are really endless.

The ancient coin field is one which has been long researched and given rise to innumerable fine books and monographs. But for all this, and despite a gradual drying up of better material, prices today remain quite reasonable. For example, a representative series of the various Roman emperors can still be acquired for less than some series' of regular issue U.S. coins. Of course, prices *have* gone up since 1964, as a few examples among both the commoner and rarer items illustrate.

	1964	1970
Macedon. Alex. the Great. Tetradrachm. V.F.	$ 45.00	$ 75.00
Alex. the Great. Gold stater. V.F.	200.00	350.00
Athens. Tetradrachm. 5th century B.C. V.F.	65.00	100.00
Syracuse. Decadrachm. V.F.	3,100.00	4,000.00
Rome. Gordianus III. Antoninianus. V.F.	4.50	7.00
Marcus Aurelius. Gold aureus. F.D.C.	525.00	900.00

In Mr. Schulman's opinion, the gradual lessening of archaeological discoveries together with a continued upsurge of collector interest will eventually send ancient coin prices skyrocketing. We have already had a foretaste of this with respect to the Judaean silver coins and the rarer Greek and Roman gold issues. Doubtless, it is only a matter of time before the commoner silver type coins follow suit.

I have already mentioned primitive money, and I would now like to call attention to this interesting field as a good possibility for long-term investment. For one thing, it is still very much depressed and offers opportunities for acquisition that will be unheard of a few years hence. For another, with the gradual acculturation of the primitive peoples of the world, their classical artifacts, including money, are no longer being made. Finally, as the older collections are being disposed of, their contents are more often than not purchased by some museum or foundation.

As I write this, I have before me a catalogue of the fabulous Gibbs collection which was auctioned off last year by Mr. Shulman. This was undoubtedly the greatest collection of primitive money ever amassed by any single person or institution, and will serve as an excellent primer for new students in the field.

What is primitive money? Anything other than coins or paper currency that has ever functioned as a medium of exchange anywhere in the world; more specifically, various shell beads and strung animal teeth, certain feathers, rings and bracelets, elephant tail bristles, ancient Chinese tea bricks, particular cloth articles, tools, weapons and ever so many other curious things. The field is virtually inexhaustible, and offers one of the most fascinating educational hobbies I can imagine.

Appendix

The following is a list of the various coin dealers with whom I have had satisfactory business transactions over the years, and who are still active in the business. As many of those listed are not regular advertisers to the numismatic journals, their inclusion will hopefully be of use to the old as well as the new collector.

ALABAMA

Anderson News Co., 4320 Huntsville Rd., Florence, Ala. (205-766-3789)
   A leading jobber of numismatic books and supplies.

ARIZONA

Harry M. Coleman. Box 3032, Tucson, Ariz. 85702.
   U.S. paper money specialist.

ARKANSAS

James Belford. Box 649, Stuttgart, Ark. 72160 (501-922-4490)
   Specialist in U.S. silver dollars.

CALIFORNIA

International Gold Corp., Steve Markoff and Keith Fey. 4640 Hollywood Blvd., Los Angeles, Calif. 90027 (800-421-0290, toll free outside of Calif., 213-660-2090)
   One of the world's largest dealers in U.S. and foreign gold coins. Weekly gold market letter issued upon request.

A-Mark Coin Co., Steve Markoff. Address as previous.
   General numismatics.

Western Numismatics, Steve Markoff and Robert Hughes. Address as previous.

    Rare U.S. coins and proof sets, a leading B.U. roll specialist.

Superior Stamp & Coin Co., Ira and Harold Goldberg. 517 W. 7th St., Los Angeles, Calif. 90014 (213-627-2621)

    Rare U.S. and general coins, antiquities.

Forecaster Publishers, John Kamin. 1329 W. 7th St., Los Angeles, Calif. 90017 (213-483-3979)

    One of the nation's largest wholesale coin brokers; oldest and largest publishers of a weekly monetary review, including coin charts, teletype wholesale prices, sample on request.

Lawrence S. Goldberg. 1581 Roxbury Dr., Los Angeles, Calif. 90035 (213-627-2621)

    General numismatics.

Century Stamp & Coin Co., Ray Lundgren. 450 S. Hill St. and 506 W. 7th St. Los Angeles, Calif. (213-626-2732 and 626-4027)

    General numismatics, political items and western Americana.

J. W. Robinson Co. (Coin Dept.), 7th, Hope & Grand, Los Angeles, Calif. 90017 (213-MA 8-0333, Ext. 527)

    General numismatics and supplies.

J. W. Robinson Co. (Coin Dept.), 8501 Van Nuys Blvd., Panorama City, Los Angeles, Calif. 91402 (213-894-7131)

    General numismatics and supplies.

J. W. Robinson Co. (Coin Dept.), 9900 Wilshire Blvd., Beverly Hills, Calif. 90210 (213-CR 5-5464, Ext. 276)

    General numismatics and supplies.

Abner Kreisberg Corp., Abner Kreisberg and Jerry Cohen, 344 N. Beverly Dr., Beverly Hills, Calif. 90210 (213-271-4281)

    One of the nation's leading dealers in rare U.S. and foreign coins, public auctions.

Bowers and Ruddy Galleries, Inc., Q. David Bowers and James Ruddy. 6922 Hollywood Blvd., Suite 810, Hollywood, Calif. 90028 (213-466-4595)

> One of the nation's leading dealers in rare U.S. coins and patterns, also modern foreign coins and books. Publishers of the *Rare Coin Review,* a monthly bulletin (sample on request), and *Photograde.*

Downey Coin Center, Joel D. Rettew. 7848 Florence Ave., Downey, Calif. 90240 (213-927-1313)

> General numismatics, specializing in silver dollars, coin novelties.

Coin-a-Rama, George Ray. 13304 Inglewood Ave., Hawthorne, Calif. 90250 (213-679-9151)

> General numismatics.

Hawthorne Coin Shop, Harry Weber. 4407 W. El Segundo, Hawthorne, Calif. 90250 (213-676-3958)

> General numismatics.

Jonathan's Coin, Inc. 525 W. Manchester Blvd., Inglewood, Calif. 90301 (213-674-3330)

> General numismatics.

Pacific Coast Coin Exchange, Lou Carabini. 3711 Long Beach Blvd., Long Beach, Calif. 90807 (213-426-9379)

> A leading dealer in bags of silver coins, foreign gold and other investment items.

Trader Sam, Sam Frudakis. 309 E. Ocean Ave. Longbeach, Calif. 90802 (213-435-3800)

> General numismatics, especially rare gold and paper money.

George Boyd. 8413 La Palma, Buena Park, Calif. 90620 (714-522-2951)

> General numismatics.

Foothill Coins. 7728 Foothill Blvd., Tujunga, Calif. 91042 (213-352-3466)
General numismatics and supplies.

J. W. Robinson Co. (Coin Dept.), 777 E. Colorado, Pasadena, Calif. 91101 (213-SY 5-6871, Ext. 392)
General numismatics and supplies.
Danny B. Crabb. 6572 Van Nuys Blvd., Van Nuys, Calif. 91401 (213-786-0272, 786-0385)
General numismatics.

Ronald J. Gillio. 14545 Victory Blvd., Suite 400, Van Nuys, Calif. 91401 (213-873-2629)
General numismatics, western Americana.

Donald Benge. 1122 Burbank Blvd., Burbank, Calif. 91502
Silver dollar specialist.

Sylvia Haffner. Box 2153 Sta. A., La Mesa, Calif. 92041 (714-465-3968)
Foreign coins, specializing in coins of Israel.

Continental Coin, Todd Parker. 5651 Lankershim Blvd., N. Hollywood, Calif. 91601 (213-980-4736)
General numismatics.

Old Coin Shop, Harlan White. 2425 El Cajon Blvd., San Diego, Calif. 92104 (714-298-8211)
General numismatics.

The May Co. (Coin Dept.) Mission Valley Center—1702 Camino del Rio, San Diego, Calif. 92110 (714-CY 7-2511)
General numismatics and supplies.

Ed's Coin Shop, Edward B. Smolinski. Box 22, Palm Desert, Calif. 92260 (714-346-8891)
General numismatics.

A. Kosoff, Inc., Abe Kosoff. Box 4009, Palm Springs, Calif. 92262 (714-327-0158)
> One of the nation's leading dealers in rare U.S. coins and patterns; public auctions including some of the biggest name sales.

Fred Coops Stamps & Coins, Fred Coops, Jr. 457 N. "E" St., San Bernardino, Calif. 92401 (714-885-2507)
> General numismatics, books.

Bob Gamson. 488 E. 17th St., Costa Mesa, Calif. 92627 (714-548-5707)
> General numismatics.

J. W. Robinson (Coin Dept.), 2 Courts of Fashion, Newport Beach, Calif. 92660 (714-644-2800, Ext. 310)
> General numismatics and supplies.

Dick's Coin Shop. 1616 S. Chester Ave., Bakersfield, Calif. 93304 (804-832-2290)
> General numismatics.

Jim Hodge. Box 116, Santa Susana, Calif. 93063 (213-786-0385)
> General numismatics.

William Lee. 69 Plaza Center, Fresno, Calif. (209-237-5594)
> General U.S., especially Indian cents.

Gold Investments Inc. 2005 Lombard St., San Francisco, Calif. 94123 (415-563-5231)
> U.S. and foreign gold specialists.

The Emporium Downtown (Coin Dept.), 835 Market St., San Francisco, Calif. 94103 (415 YU 2-1111, Ext. 1553)
> General numismatics and supplies.

William Hall Coins. 3166 16th St., San Francisco, Calif. 94103 (415-864-6630)
> General Numismatics.

Cash Coins, William Preston. 309 Hyde St., San Francisco, Calif. 94109 (415-673-4748, 673-2350)
General numismatics.

Arnold Rosing. 181 Second Ave., San Mateo, Calif. 94401 (415-342-9711)
Specializes in U.S. and foreign gold and crowns of the world.

Aldo Basso. 2309 S. El Camino, San Mateo, Calif. 94403 (415-341-3925)
Specializes in coinage of the Philippines.

Camino Coin Co., Burt Blumert. 5 W. 37th Ave., San Mateo, Calif. 94403 (415-341-2925, 341-7991)
Rare U.S. coins, a leading dealer in U.S. gold, silver dollars and English sovereigns.

Gary L. Young. 420 17th St., Oakland, Calif. 94612 (415-444-4343)
General numismatics, a specialist in mint errors and U.S. type coins.

Marcus Reaves. 224 N. Santa Cruz, Los Gatos, Calif. 95030 (408-354-3869)
General numismatics.

San Jose Coin Shop, John Serpa. 642 Town & Country Village, San Jose, Calif. 95128 (408-244-7305)
Silver dollar specialist.

Central Stamp and Coin, John Whitehead. 905 "J" St., Modesto, Calif. 95354 (209-523-2520)
General numismatics.

Village Coin, Bob Sisson. 647 Coddington Town Center, Santa Rosa, Calif. 95401 (707-544-1621)
General numismatics.

Capitol City Coin Center. 2220 "J" St., Sacramento, Calif. 95816
(916-444-6312)
> General numismatics.

Common to Key Coin Co., Darvin Reiswig. 4431 Freeport Blvd.,
Sacramento, Calif. 95822 (916-451-5698)
> General numismatics.

COLORADO

Dan Brown's Coin Shop, Inc. 1532 Broadway, Denver Colo. 80202
(303-244-7222)
> General numismatics, especially U.S. type coins.

May, D. F. (Coin Dept.) 16th & Tremont, Denver, Colo. 80202
(303-292-8380)
> General numismatics, supplies.

Walter Laub. 1532 Broadway, Denver, Colo. 80202 (303-244-
9005)
> B.U. rolls of U.S. coins.

L & L Coins, Roger Loecher and Vern Lowe. #20 Lakeside
Shopping Center, 5801 W. 44th Ave., Denver, Colo. 80212 (303-
455-6941)
> General numismatics.

Tebo Coin Co. Box T, 1136 Spruce, Boulder, Colo. 80302 (303-
444-2426)
> U.S. coins and currency.

Al C. Overton. Box 967, Colorado Springs, Colo. 80901
> General U.S. coins, a leading specialist in early half dollars.

CONNECTICUT

Connecticut Valley Coin Co., Edwin E. Blow. 97 Center St., Manchester, Conn. 06040 (203-643-6295)
> General numismatics.

G. Fox & Co. (Coin Dept.), 960 Main St., Hartford, Conn. 06115 (203-249-9711, Ext. 8020)
General numismatics, supplies.

Silver City Coin Co., Walter Lukashevich. 29 Colony St., Meriden, Conn. 06450 (203-235-7634)
General numismatics.

Benjamin Levin. 514 W. Taft Ave., Bridgeport, Conn. 06604
General numismatics, rare gold coins.

Sam Sloat. 136 M. St., Westport, Conn. 06880 (203-226-4279)
General U.S., especially silver dollars.

DELAWARE

Hance Jaquett. 810 Orange St., Wilmington, Del. 19801
General numismatics.

DISTRICT OF COLUMBIA

Jack Martin. 722 11th St., N.W. Washington, D.C. 20001 (202-628-3071)
General numismatics.

Woodward & Lothrop (Coin Dept.), 11th & F Sts. N.W. Washington, D.C. 20013 (202-347-5300, Ext. 412 & 511)
General numismatics and supplies.

FLORIDA

G.B.H., Ltd., 500-B Main St., Box 3686, Daytona Beach, Fla. 32018 (904-252-0874)
General numismatics.

Edgewood Coin Shop, Emory M. Robinson. 934 S. Edgewood Ave., Box 6576, Jacksonville, Fla. 32205 (904-389-0013)
General numismatics.

Grover C. Criswell. Rt. 2, Box 1085, Citra, Fla. 32627
A leading specialist in Confederate and southern state currency and bonds.

G. G. Finnell Coin Sales, Inc., Gerald G. Finnell. P.O. Box 6063-C, Orlando, Fla. 32814 (305-424-0796)
General U.S. coins, supplies, a leading book dealer.

Pompano Collector's Corner, Benjamin Dreiske. 2433 E. Atlantic Blvd., Pompano Beach, Fla. 33062
General numismatics.

Trend Coin Co., Al and J. Weinberg. 8990 Biscayne Blvd., Miami, Fla. 33138 (305-758-5506)
General U.S., bulk silver coins, foreign gold.

William Youngerman, Inc. Box 3043 Norland Branch, Miami, Fla. 33169 (305-624-3007)
U.S. and foreign gold.

Louis A. Montesi. 12953 Biscayne Blvd., North Miami, Fla. 33161 (305-891-1806)
General numismatics.

Robert Steinberg. Box 7255, Ft. Lauderdale, Fla. 33304 (305-781-3455)
Rare coins, U.S. and foreign gold specialist.

Jack C. Keeton, Jr. 2745 Broadway, Box 10502, Riviera Beach, Fla. 33404 (305-844-7710)
General numismatics.
French's, Charles and Arline French. Box 256, Jensen Beach, Fla. 33457 (305-287-1566)
General numismatics, auctions.

Joe Person. 445 1st Ave., No. St. Petersburg, Fla. 33731 (813-898-6779)
General numismatics.

Allen's Coin Shop, Lawrence L. Allen. 2235 Fowler St., Ft. Myers, Fla. 33901 (813-936-4653)
General numismatics.

GEORGIA

World-Wide Coin Investments, Inc., John Hamrick. Box 681, Atlanta, Ga. 30301 (404-523-5388)
> General numismatics, especially type coins, commemoratives, proof sets and B.U. rolls.

Rich's (Coin Dept.), Broad at Alabama, Atlanta, Ga. 30302 (404-JA 2-4636, Ext. 8264)
> General numismatics, supplies.

HAWAII

Gordon Medcalf. 1236 Ala Moana Center, Honolulu, Hawaii 96814
> Specialist in Hawaiian coins.

ILLINOIS

Marshall Field and Co. (Coin Dept.), One Old Orchard, Skokie, Ill. 60076 (312-674-1234, Ext. 663)
> General numismatics, supplies.

Tom Ryan. 123 Yorktown, Lombardo, Ill. 60148 (312-629-7575)
> Rare coins, currency and general numismatics.

Ralph Graf. 60 W. Madison St., Chicago, Ill. 60602 (312-372-1925)
> Specialist in B.U. rolls.

Rarcoa, David J. Shapiro. 31 North Clark St., Chicago, Ill. 60602 (312-346-3443)
> Rare U.S. and foreign coins, public auctions.

Gold Stella Coin Co., Edward Milas. 112 South Dearborn St., Chicago, Ill. 60603 (312-641-2688)
> U.S. gold rarities.

Beverly Hills Coin Shop, Inc., Larry Whitlow. N-9 Evergreen Plaza, Evergreen Park, Ill. 60642 (312-422-5100)
> General numismatics.

Kraso Coins, Witold E. Krasowski. 2349 W. 95th St., Chicago, Ill. 60643 (312-239-1461)
General numismatics.

Strauss Coin Co., Inc., Edwin B. Strauss. 3111 W. Devon Ave., Chicago, Ill. 60645 (312-274-0124)
General numismatics.

Marshall Field and Co. (Coin Dept.), 111 N. State St., Chicago, Ill. 60690 (312-ST 1-1000, Ext. 2281)
General numismatics, supplies.

Illini House, Ray Kotansky. Box 438, Streator, Ill. 61344 (815-672-1698)
A leading dealer in bags of silver coins.

Fred Vollmer. Box 88, Bloomington, Ill. 61701 (309-827-6051)
General U.S., specializing in silver dollars and gold coins; one of the leading proof set dealers.

Jess Peters, Inc., Box 123 Decatur, Ill. 62525 (217-428-2074)
Specialist in foreign crowns.

INDIANA

Pollard Coin & Stamp Supply Co., Wilson E. Pollard. Box 18095, Indianapolis, Ind. 46218 (317-547-1306)
General numismatics, a leading jobber of supplies.

L. S. Ayres & Co. (Coin Dept.), 1 W. Washington St., Indianapolis, Ind. 46204 (317-ME 7-4411, Ext. 380)
General numismatics, supplies.

Winchester Coin Shop's Silver Towne, Leon B. Hendrickson. Box 424, Winchester, Ind. 47394.
A leading dealer in bags of silver coins, U.S. gold, commemoratives, English sovereigns, and silver bars.

IOWA

Hollinbeck-Kagin Co., Arthur and Paul Kagin, Suite 400, Royal Union Bldg., Des Moines, Iowa 50309 (515-244-3179)
> One of the nation's leading U.S. coin dealers. Specialists in exceptionally rare coins, patterns and currency. Mail bid auctions, catalogues on request.

A & A Coins, Inc., Dean Oakes. Box 469, Iowa City, Iowa 52240 (319-338-1424)
> General numismatics, U.S. paper money specialist.

KANSAS

Joe Flynn Sr. Coin Co., Inc., Joe Flynn Sr. & Jr. 2854 W. 47th St. Box 3997, Kansas City, Kan. 66103 (913-236-7171)
> Rare U.S. coins specialist, price list issued on request.

Heart of America, Hurley Cook and Larry Shepard. 1729 Stewart St., Kansas City, Kan. 66104 (913-371-7779)
> General numismatics.

Jack L. Klausen. 3239 No. 66 Terrace, Kansas City, Kan. 66104 (913-299-3293)
> General numismatics, U.S. rarities.

The House of Stuart, Ltd., Gary Sturtbridge. 1 Gateway Center, Suite 100, Kansas City, Kan. 66117 (913-371-1680)
> General numismatics, U.S. type coins.

Leasure's Treasure Chest, Elden Leasure. Box 304, Manhattan, Kansas 66502 (913-778-5233)
> General numismatics.

B & B Coin, Inc., George D. Benge. 730½ Kansas Ave., Topeka, Kan. 66603 (913-232-2861)
> General numismatics.

Smies' Coin Shop, Inc., John J. Smies. Box 66, Courtland, Kan. 66939 (913-374-3421)
General numismatics.

KENTUCKY

The Numismatic Exchange, Byrd Saylor, Jr. 214 S. Third St. Louisville, Ky. 40202 (502-584-9879)
General numismatics.

James, Inc., D. W. Karp. Box 18088, Louisville, Ky. 40218 (502-583-4851)
General numismatics.

LOUISIANA

Maison Blanche Co. (Coin Dept.), 901 Canal, New Orleans, La. 70160 (504-522-3434, Ext. 231)
General numismatics, supplies.

SeRo Coins, Inc., Jack Setzer and James Rosenbloom. Box 5567-N, Shreveport, La. 71105
Specialists in Mexican gold coins.

MARYLAND

Woodward & Lothrop (Coin Dept.), Wisconsin & Western, Chevy Chase, Md. 20015 (301-654-7600, Ext. 215)
General numismatics and supplies.

Frank & Laurese Katen. P.O. Box 4047, Colesville Sta., Silver Spring, Md. 20904 (301-384-9444)
A leading specialist in numismatic literature.

Julian Leidman. 8439 Georgia Ave., Silver Spring, Md. 20910 (301-585-8467)
Extremely rare U.S. coins and paper money.

Hutzler's (Coin Dept.), 212 N. Howard St., South Blvd., Baltimore, Md. 21201 (301-727-1234)
General numismatics and supplies.

MASSACHUSETTS

Crystal Coin Co., Bill Scott, Ed. J. Carr. 351 Main St., Box 234, Wakefield, Mass. 01881 (617-245-0014)
    General numismatics.

Jordan Marsh Co. (Coin Dept.), 450 Washington St., Boston, Mass. 02107 (617-426-9000, Ext. 2842)
    General numismatics, supplies.

J. J. Teaparty, 43 Bromfield St., Boston, Mass. 02108
    General numismatics, paper money, U.S. type coins.

Michael R. Kirzner. 44 Bromfield St., Boston, Mass. 02108 (617-482-6498)
    Rare U.S. coins, patterns, fractional currency.

Ralph Goldstone. 581 Boylston St., Boston, Mass. 02116 (617-266-6004)
    Specialist in Colonial coins, U.S. paper money, foreign crowns and political items.

John Frates. 102 W. Center St., W. Bridgewater, Mass. 02379
    General numismatics.

MICHIGAN

Coin Investments, Inc., John Abbott. 725 S. Adams Rd., Birmingham, Mich. 48012 (313-642-5081)
    A leading specialist in U.S. and foreign gold coins.

Coins and Stamps, Inc., R. F. Lester. 17658 Mack Ave., Grosse Pointe, Mich. 48224 (313-885-4200)
    General numismatics, especially U.S. silver dollars.

The J. L. Hudson Co. (Coin Dept.), 1206 Woodward Ave., Detroit, Mich. 48226 (313-223-5100, Ext. 2080 & 2092)
    General numismatics and supplies.

Earl Schill. 1434 Farmer St., Detroit, Mich. 48226 (313-961-1333)
  General numismatics.

International Coin Exchange, Joel Overstreet. 5495 State Rd., Saginaw, Mich. 48603 (517-792-4211)
  General numismatics.

Numismatic Investment Corp., Al Spaeth. State Bank Blvd., Rm. C., Bay Port, Mich. 48720 (313-875-2260)
  General numismatics, especially B.U. rolls.

MINNESOTA

Johnny Adams, Jr. Box 308. Wayzata, Minn. 55391 (612-473-7848)
  General numismatics.

Tonka Hobby Supply. Box 166, Wayzata, Minn. 55391.
  General books and supplies.

William Ulrich Sr. and Jr. P. O. Box 22476, Minneapolis, Minn. 55427 (612-544-0936)
  Rare U.S. and foreign coins.

Dayton's (Coin Dept.), 700 on the Mall, Minneapolis, Minn. 55402 (612-FE 2-6123, Ext. 2366)
  General numismatics, supplies.

National Coin Studios, Jeff Munger and Dennis Heller. 415 Lincoln Bank Bldg., Minneapolis, Minn. 55403 (612-333-3569)
  General numismatics.

Dean C. Johnson. Box 27094, 8134 34th Ave., No. Crystal, Minn. 55427 (612-544-8953)
  General numismatics.

Bill Mertes. 605 N. 7th Ave., St. Cloud, Minn. 56301 (612-252-6232)
  General numismatics.

MISSOURI

Famous-Barr Co. (Coin Dept.), 6th & Olive, St. Louis, Mo. 63101 (314-421-5900)
General numismatics and supplies.

Mid-Continent Coin Co., W. L. (Dutch) Rhoning. 308 E. 12th St., Kansas City, Mo. 64106 (816-842-7888)
General numismatics.

Fred Sweeney, Inc. Box 10144, Kansas City, Mo. 64111 (816-753-5860)
General numismatics, paper money, U.S. type coins.

MONTANA

Record Coin Shop, John B. Love. 13 S. Central, Box 167, Cut Bank, Montana 59427 (406-938-4263)
General numismatics, a leading dealer in B.U. U.S. silver dollars.

NEBRASKA

Brandeis (Coin Dept.), 16th & Douglas, Omaha, Nebr. 68102 (402-341-8666, Ext. 542)
General numismatics, supplies.

Bebee's, Inc., Aubrey E. Bebee. 4514 No. 30th St., Omaha, Nebr. 68111 (402-451-4766)
General numismatics, one of the leading dealers in commemoratives and an owner of one of the fabulous 1913 Liberty head nickels. Also, a leading jobber of books and supplies.

NEVADA

U-Namit-Collector's Shop, Lee Steiger. P.O. Box 837, Henderson, Nev. 89015 (702-564-2157)
General numismatics.

Fremont Coin Co., Inc., Phil Carlino. 313 E. Fremont St., Las Vegas, Nevada 89101 (702-382-1469)
General numismatics.

Stan Zurowski. 2409 Las Vegas Blvd., S., Las Vegas, Nevada 89105 (702-735-2022, 735-2051)
One of the leading dealers in U.S. silver dollars.

Eddie Doyle. P.O. Box 5151, Airport, Las Vegas, Nevada 89111 (305-782-2383)
General numismatics, especially B.U. rolls.

Ace Coin Co., Joe Meyers. 355 N. Virginia St., Reno, Nevada 89501 (702-323-3303)
General numismatics, especially U.S. silver dollars.

Consolidated Coin Co., Frank Roza, Jr. P.O. Box 1406, Carson City, Nevada 89701 (702-882-6277)
General U.S., specialist in gold, silver dollars, and Carson City mint coins.

NEW HAMPSHIRE

Nashua Coin & Stamp. Tony Gouveia and Louis Brand. 168 Main St., Nashua, N.H. 03060 (603-889-6312)
General numismatics.

Melvin E. Came & Son. 4 Hillcrest Dr., Dover, N.H. 03820 (603-742-3320)
Rare Canadian, foreign and U.S. coins.

NEW JERSEY

Plainfield Coin Center, John Troyan, Jr. 411 Park Ave., Plainfield, N.J. 07060 (201-753-9469)
General numismatics, type coins, silver bar specialist.

Colony Coin Shop, Ron Friedman. 106 Elm St., Westfield, N.J. 07090 (201- 233-5411)
General numismatics.

Criterion Coin Center, Frank Roth. Wayne, N.J. 07470 (201-891-5379)
General numismatics.

Charles H. McSorley. Box 21, Closter, N.J. 07624 (201-768-2064)
   Ancient coins, U.S. and political rarities.

Gimbels (Coin Dept.), Garden State Plaza, Paramaus, N.J. 07652
(201-843-9400, Ext. 278)
   General numismatics and supplies.

East Coast Coin Co. 264 Highway 35, Eatontown, N.J. 07724
   (201-542-2091)
   General U.S. coins, especially B.U. rolls and proof sets.

Madison Coin Box, Inc. Edward L. Hilbert. 34 Lincoln Place,
Madison, N.J. 07940 (201-377-1077)
   General numismatics.

Henry Christensen. P.O. Box 1732, Madison, N.J. 07940 (201-
656-2266)
   Latin American coins specialist, public auctions held.

Phil Saxton. Berlin Farmers Market, Berlin, N.J. (609-767-0775)
   General numismatics.

Charles (Chuck) O'Donnell. Rt. 3, Box 123, Williamtown, N.J.
08094 (609-629-5160)
   A leading specialist in U.S. paper money, including current
   federal reserve notes.

Penn Jersey Coin Exchange. 614 W. Maple Ave., Merchantville,
N.J. 08109 (609-662-2615)
   General numismatics.

Pep's Coin Vault/Pep Levin, Inc. Box 69, Pennsauken, N.J. (215-
467-4148)
   A leading dealer in new and junk bags of silver coins.

NEW MEXICO

J. Addison Cammack. 1500 S. Ave., D., Box 4147, Portales, New Mexico 88130 (505-356-5080)

NEW YORK

Capitol Coin Co., Jack Friedberg. 393 Seventh Ave., New York City, N.Y. 10001 (212-947-0370)
One of the nation's leading wholesale dealers in general U.S. and foreign coins, and supplies.

Gimbels (Coin Dept.) 33rd St. & Broadway, New York City, N.Y. 10001 (212-564-3300, Ext. 375-376)
General numismatics, supplies.

Federal Coins and Currency, Inc. 25 Broad St., Rm. 425, New York City, N.Y. 10004 (212-943-4141)
A leading dealer in bags of silver coins and gold coins for investment purposes.

Medallic Art Co., William T. Louth. 325 E. 45th St., New York City, N.Y. 10017 (212-679-1616)
Manufacturers of medals.

J. J. Van Grover. Box 200, Midtown Sta., New York City, N.Y. 10018 (212-224-9578)
Specialist in the coins of Israel.

Coen-Messer Co., Daniel Messer. 39 W. 55th St., New York City, N.Y. 10019 (212-246-5025)
General numismatics.

Stacks. 123 W. 57th St., New York City, N.Y. 10019 (212-582-2580)
One of the nation's leading dealers in rare U.S. coins. Public auctions including many of the biggest name sales. Has subsidiary (Coin Galleries) at same address (212-582-5955), which is a leading dealer in foreign and ancient coins. Publishes the *Numismatic Review*.

Manfra, Tordella & Brooks, Inc. 59 W. 49th St., New York City, N.Y. 10020 (212-757-9670)
   General numismatics, antiquities and foreign exchange.

Max L. Kaplan. 663 5th Ave., New York City, N.Y. 10022 (212-753-4588)
   Rare U.S. coins, especially silver and gold.

Lester Merkin. 65 E. 56th St., New York City, N.Y. 10022.
   A leading dealer in rare U.S. coins and paper money, public auctions.

Theodore Kemm. 915 W. End Ave., New York City, N.Y. 10025 (212-864-6164)
   Specialist in U.S. paper money.

New Netherlands Coin Co., Charles M. Wormser. 1 W. 47th St., New York City, N.Y. 10036 (212-757-5245)
   A leading dealer in rare U.S. coins, tokens and paper money. Public auctions, including some big name sales.

Schulman Coin and Mint, Inc., Hans M. F. Schulman. 25 W. 45th St., New York City, N.Y. 10036 (212-687-3145)
   A leading dealer in foreign and ancient coins, primitive money and antiquities. Public auctions including many big name sales. Also manufactures medals. A publicly held company.

Donald Brigandi. 103 W. 45th St., New York City, N.Y. 10036 (212-582-7160)
   General numismatics.

Graf & Sons. 128 W. 45th St., New York City, N.Y. 10036 (212-265-4691)
   General numismatics.

Maurice Geiger. 47 N. 47th St., New York City, N.Y. 10036 (212-246-9257)
   General numismatics.

Caro-len Coin Co., Milton Dinkin. 149 W. 44th St., New York City, N.Y. 10036 (212-581-1127)
General numismatics, especially political items.

Alan J. Rosenberg, Inc. Box 436, Peck Slip Sta., New York City, N.Y. 10038 (212-544-3477)
General U.S., a leading dealer in bags of silver coins.

Aaron Feldman. Box 854, Ansonia Sta., New York City, N.Y. 10023 (212-362-9517)
A leading dealer in numismatic literature, especially rare and out-of-date works.

Jerry Leavitt. Box 59 H, Scarsdale, N.Y. 10583
Choice U.S. coins, especially commemoratives.

Yonkers Coin Exchange, Jerry Moskowitz and Pat Macia. 95 Marmaroneck, White Plains, N.Y. 10601 (914-761-3240-1)
General numismatics.

Gimbels (Coin Dept.), Cross Country Shopping Center, Yonkers, N.Y. 10704 (914-963-8000, Ext. 278)
General numismatics, supplies.

Franklin Square Coin Co., Robert M. Jenove. Box 101-T, Franklin Square, N.Y. 11010.
Specialist in early U.S. silver and type coins.

Nassau County Rare Coin and Stamp, Erasmus Iannacone. 912 A Hempstead Turnpike, Franklin Square, N.Y. 11010 (516-352-7277)
General numismatics.

Brooklyn Heights Coin Exchange, John Conrad. 63 Clark St., Brooklyn, N.Y. 11201 (212-596-1262)
General U.S., especially B.U. rolls and other investment material.

Marcel Silton. Box 324, Jackson Heights, N.Y. 11372 (212-458-1950)
   Rare ancient and foreign coins.

Robert S. Ittelson. 9931 65th Rd., Rego Park, N.Y. 11374 (212-897-9503)
   General U.S. coins, proof set specialist.

William Donner Coin Co., Inc. Box 267, Forest Hills, N.Y. 11375 (212-263-1976)
   Ancient coins and U.S. and foreign gold specialist.

First Coin Investors. 16 McKinley Ave., Albertson, N.Y. 11507 (516-294-0040)
   General investment material. A publicly held company, stock sold over the counter.

Richard Picker. Box 123, Albertson, N.Y. (516-621-0763)
   A leading dealer and specialist in American colonial coins and colonial and continental currency.

J. A. Scott & Co., John Scott and John Abruscato. 955 Willis Ave., Albertson, N.Y. (516-294-0030)
   General numismatics.

Gimbels (Coin Dept.), Roosevelt Field Shopping Center, Garden City, N.Y. 11533 (516-751-6554)
   General numismatics, supplies.

John J. Ford, Jr. P.O. Box 33, Rockville Center, N.Y. 11571 (516-764-8988)
   Rare U.S. coin and paper money specialist.

Coin Guild of America, Jack Wunderman. 1525 Forest Ave., Baldwin, N.Y. 11510 (516-868-3444)
   Prime investment material. Free list on request.

M. & S. Hirschhorn, Inc. 255 Broadway, Lynbrook, N.Y. 11563 (516-593-3353)
> A leading dealer in U.S. and foreign gold, foreign crowns and B.U. rolls. Price list on request.

Intervest Coin Exchange. 255 Broadway, Lynbrook, N.Y. 11563 (516-593-3353)
> Investment counselors for all types of coins.

Jules Karp. 361 Beach 12th St., Far Rockaway, N.Y. 11691 (212-337-5300)
> General U.S., proof sets, B.U. rolls and other investment material.

Don Hirschhorn, Inc. 714-19 Sheer Plaza, Plainview, N.Y. 11803 (516-694-7520)
> One of the nation's leading jobbers of numismatic books and supplies. A publicly held corporation.

The Old Roman, Inc. 537 Mid Island Plaza, Hicksville, N.Y. 11801 (516-822-0888)
> General numismatics.

Gimbels (Coin Dept.), Green Acres Shopping Center, Valley Stream, N.Y. 11580 (516-561-6100, Ext. 278)
> General numismatics, supplies.

Blueberry Coin & Stamp Co., Ted Reich. 190 Blueberry Lane, Hicksville, N.Y. 11801 (516-433-2272)
> General numismatics.

David W. Nethaway. 4 S. Grand St., Cobleskill, N.Y. 12043 (518-234-3749)
> General numismatics.

Inter-Gold Corp., John Dowd. 15 Computer Dr., West, Albany, N.Y. 12205 (518-459-4048)
> One of the world's leading dealers in foreign gold, especially English sovereigns; also junk silver coins. Offers daily gold coin quotations.

Jonah Shapiro. 1027 University Bldg., Syracuse, N.Y. 13202 (315-474-6517)
　　Coins of Israel specialist; also general numismatics including ancients.

William P. Donlon. Box 144, Utica, N.Y. 13503 (315-735-2525)
　　U.S. paper money specialist.

Joe Kuehnert. Box 5, Sta. "G," Buffalo, N.Y. 14213 (716-873-5279)
　　General numismatics.

John E. Nelson. Box 999, Jamestown, N.Y. 14701 (716-487-0759)
　　General numismatics.

NORTH CAROLINA

Tar Heel Coin Co. 45 2nd St., Drive N.E. Hickory, N.C. (704-323-4652)
　　General numismatics.

OHIO

Lazarus & Co. (Coin Dept.), High and Town Sts., Columbus, Ohio 43216 (614-463-3257)
　　General numismatics, supplies.

C. C. Shroyer. Box 424, Fremont, Ohio 43420 (419-332-3224)
　　General U.S., especially commemorative coins.

Charles H. Wolfe. Box 222, Lakeside, Ohio 43440 (419-798-4582)
　　General numismatics.

Brysons Coin Co., Don and By Place. 612 White St., Toledo, Ohio 43605 (419-691-3407)
　　Specializes in type coins in all conditions.

Ed's Coins, Ed Clemente. 3725 Williston Rd., Woodwill Mall, Toledo, Ohio 43616 (419-691-9102)
General U.S., especially proof sets.

Hy Brown. 185 Main St., Painsville, Ohio 44077 (216-357-5544)
General U.S. coins, specializing in commemoratives and silver bars.

Art-Gem Coins. 79-16 Harvard, Cleveland, Ohio 44105 (216-341-5195)
General numismatics.

Higbee's (Coin Dept.), 100 Public Square, Cleveland, Ohio 44113 (216-579-7391, Ext. 414)
General numismatics, supplies.

Alan Cohen, Jr. 15 Colonial Arcade, Cleveland, Ohio 44115 (216-241-6826)
General numismatics.

Shaker Coin Shop, Inc. Louis M. Irwin. 20320 Farnsleigh Rd., Shaker Heights, Ohio 44122 (216-295-1755)
General numismatics.

World Coin Co., Renato Montorsi. 6865 Southland Dr., Cleveland, Ohio 44130 (216-842-5242)
General numismatics.

Federal Brand, Michael Kolman, Jr. 5940 Pearl Rd., Parma Heights, Ohio 44130 (216-844-0701)
General numismatics.

Southland Coin Corp., Jim Hausknecht. 6809 W. 130th, Cleveland, Ohio 44130 (216-845-0600)
General numismatics.

Harry Jones. Box 42043, Brookpark, Ohio 44142 (216-234-4340)
General U.S., specializing in currency errors and B.U. rolls.

Dick Krotz. 691 Richmond Rd., Richmond Mall, Cleveland, Ohio 44143 (216-461-4411)
General numismatics.

Harold Berk. 2671 Youngstown Rd., Warren, Ohio 44484 (216-369-1192)
General numismatics.

Pogue's (Coin Dept.), 5th St. Bldg., Cincinnati, Ohio 45202 (513-381-4700)
General numismatics, supplies.

Sol Kaplan. 1103 Transit Bldg., 6 East Fourth St., Cincinnati, Ohio 45202 (513-621-2998)
Specialist in U.S. patterns, proof sets, commemoratives and other rare items.

Steve Eyer. 13 Lakeshore Dr., Cincinnati, Ohio 45237 (513-761-7832)
General numismatics.

Paramount International Coin Corp., Max J. Humbert and Hon. Michael V. DiSalle. Paramount Bldg., Dept. 1, Englewood, Ohio 45322 (513-836-2654)
One of the nation's leading dealers in rare U.S. and foreign coins. Public auctions, monthly price list issued on request. A publicly held corporation.

Robert M. Ullrich. 1 N. Main St., Englewood, Ohio 45322 (513-836-1711)
General numismatics.

Presidential Art Medals, Inc., Frank Darner. 10 W. National Rd., Englewood, Ohio 45322 (513-836-3635)
A medal manufacturer.

Phil Lampkin. Box 37312, Cincinnati, Ohio 45327
A U.S. paper money specialist.

Cline's Coins. 3718 Salem Ave., Dayton, Ohio 45406 (513-274-9200)
> General U.S., especially type coins.

Redman's Dayton Mall Shop. Rm. 1142, Dayton Mall, Dayton, Ohio 45459 (513-433-9607)
> General U.S., a silver dollar specialist.

OKLAHOMA

Bob's Coin Shop, Bob Wilson. 123 N. Washington, Enid, Okla. 73701 (405-237-2371)
> General numismatics.

OREGON

Meier & Frank (Coin Dept.), 5th, 6th, Morrison & Adler, Portland, Oregon 97204 (503-227-4411)
> General numismatics, supplies.

Norman Locke. 407 S.W. Washington, Portland, Ore. 97204 (503-223-0335)
> General numismatics.

PENNSYLVANIA

T. H. Young. 111 Fineview Dr., Beaver Falls, Pa. 15010 (412-846-8355)
> General numismatics.

Kaufmann's (Coin Dept.), 400 5th Ave., Pittsburgh, Pa. 15219 (412-281-1000, Ext. 598)
> General numismatics, supplies.

Liberty Coin Shop, Frank Cafaro. Grant Building, Pittsburgh, Pa. 15219 (412-481-4862)
> General numismatics, especially silver dollars.

Ted Shiff. Box 13043, Pittsburgh, Pa. 15243 (412-276-6782)
> General numismatics.

Art Leister. Box 607, Camp Hill, Pa. 17011 (717-737-8981)
General U.S., specializing in U.S. silver dollars and rare U.S. currency.

Loser's Coin Store, John Loser. 48 Kline Village, Harrisburg, Pa. 17104 (717-238-9184)
General numismatics.

Robert P. Faust. 54 Beaver, York, Pa. 17401 (717-854-9468)
General numismatics.

Ken Seachman. 44 W. Market St., York, Pa. 17401 (717-854-9339)
General numismatics.

Charles R. Heisler, Inc., 500 Oak Grove Dr., Lancaster, Pa. 17601 (717-393-3061)
A leading jobber of coin supplies, books.

Montgomery Coin Co., Ed Gorlin. Rt. 309, Montgomeryville, Pa. (215-855-1542)
General numismatics.

Ossie's Coin Shop, Vernon H. Oswald. 1013 Hamilton St., Allentown, Pa. 18101 (215-433-4474)
General U.S. coins, a paper money specialist.

Gerry Gelone. Quakertown Farmers Market, Quakertown, Pa. (215-723-9576)
General numismatics.

R. N. Matylewicz. 718 E. Elm St., Scranton, Penna. 18505
U.S. coins and currency.

Robert F. Batchelder. 1 W. Butler Ave., Ambler, Pa. 19002 (215-643-1430)
Rare U.S. coins, autographs.

Penn Valley Coin Shoppe, Inc., Mulford B. Simons, Jr. 22 E. Lancaster Ave., Ardmore, Pa. 19003 (215-649-7255)
General U.S., type coins.

Bernard Gimelson. Box 9, Fort Washington, Pa. 19034 (215-646-1293)
Rare U.S. coins, paper money and autographs.

Edelman's, Milton Edelman. 301 Old York Rd., Jenkintown, Pa. 19046 (215-887-7000)
General numismatics.

James Dolan. Bucks County Mall, Feasterville, Pa. 19047 (215-355-7950)
U.S. coins, rare medals and decorations.

Ed Hipps. 636 Shoparama, Levittown, Pa. 19055 (215-943-3330)
General numismatics.

Philly Stamp & Coin, Ferdnand Creed. 1804 Chestnut St., Philadelphia, Pa. 19103 (215-563-7341)
General numismatics.

Coinhunter, C. E. Bullowa. 1616 Walter St., Philadelphia, Pa. 19103 (215-735-5517)
General numismatics including ancient coins.

Gimbels (Coin Dept.), 9th at Market St., Philadelphia, Pa. 19105 (215-922-3300, Ext. 2318)
General numismatics, supplies.

Mill Dutkin Coins. 56 N. 13th St., Philadelphia, Pa. 19107 (215-563-0857)
General U.S. coins and paper money, plastic coin novelties.

Penn Coin Shop, Walter Mattner, Jr. 908 Arch St., Philadelphia, Pa. 19107 (215-922-1518)
General numismatics.

George Creed. 22 S. 10th St., Philadelphia, Pa. 19107 (215-922-6667)
General numismatics.

Allied Hobby, Jack Mealy. 6607 Rising Sun Ave., Philadelphia, Pa. 19111 (215-722-0292)
General numismatics, price list on request.

Dave's Northeast Mint, Dave Gorlin. 1825 Cottman St., Philadelphia, Pa. 19111 (215-745-4900)
General numismatics.

Normandy Square Coin Co., Dave Gorlin. Comly & Roosevelt Blvd., Philadelphia, Pa. 19115 (215-677-5066)
General numismatics.

Harry Kirschner. 1825 Allegheny, Philadelphia, Pa. 19134 (215-423-8775)
General numismatics.

Andrew Moore. Box 109, Hamburg, Pa. 19526 (215-562-4424)
General numismatics.

Frank Almond. Downingtown Farmers Market, Downingtown, Pa. (215-323-1098)
General numismatics.

Thomas E. Werner. 315 No. Matlack, West Chester, Pa. 19380
General numismatics, a specialist in U.S. fractional currency.

SOUTH CAROLINA

Candy's Coins, Bill Hodges and Bill Robinson. Box 5754-B, Greenville S.C. 29606 (803-235-2616)
General numismatics.

TENNESSEE

Chattanooga Coin Co., Gary Fillers and Doc Denton. Box 1028, Chattanooga, Tenn. 37401 (615-267-8974)
Specialists in silver dollars, commemoratives, proof sets and B.U. rolls; publishers of a monthly coin paper, the *Coin Wholesaler,* sample free upon request.

T. J. Byrd. 525 Magnolia Ave., N.E. Knoxville, Tenn. 37917 (615-522-0511)
   General numismatics.

David Pike. 2015 Madison, Memphis, Tenn. 38104 (901-275-3606)
   General numismatics.

Southeastern Coins, Pat Brewer. 301 Tennessee St., Box 111, Collinwood, Tenn. 38450 (615-724-4518)
   General numismatics.

TEXAS

Steve Ivy. 1600 L.T.V. Towers, Dallas, Texas 75201 (214-747-7391)
   General U.S. and type coins.

Thomas C. Bain. 3717 Marquette Dr., Dallas, Texas 75225
   Specialist in southern state currency.

B & B Coins and Supplies. Box 116161, Fort Worth, Texas 76133 (817-924-9745)
   General numismatics and supplies.

Douglas W. Weaver Rare Coin Co. 522 Golden Triangle, Waco, Texas 76710 (817-772-3240)
   General numismatics.

Foley's (Coin Dept.), 110 Main St., Houston, Texas 77001 (713-228-3311, Ext. 576)
   General numismatics, supplies.

Hassan A. Tulbah. 2204 W. Gray St., Houston, Texas 77019 (713-529-5881-82)
   General U.S. coins.

Colonial Coins. 373 Memorial City, Houston, Texas 77024 (713-464-3765)
   General numismatics.

Carlo Cassano. 4008 Bellaire Blvd., Houston, Texas 77025 (713-668-7125)
    General numismatics.

Astro City Coin and Stamp, Don Swanson. 6100 Westheimer, Suite 144, Houston, Texas 77027 (713-781-3048, 781-4190)
    General numismatics.

Majors Coin Co., Gene Majors. 2012 South Richey, Pasadena, Texas 77502 (713-477-2440)
    General numismatics.

Warren's Coin & Stamp Co., Cecil D. Warren, Jr. 2125 Strawberry, Pasadena, Texas 77502 (713-472-2057)
    General numismatics.

Joske's of Texas (Coin Dept.), By the Alamo, San Antonio, Texas 78206 (512-227-4343)
    General numismatics, supplies.

Robert A. Glascock. Box 8192, San Antonio, Texas 78208
    General numismatics and books.

Austin Coin Co., David Bland, Jr. 1508 Lavaca, Dept. 7, Austin, Texas 78701
    General numismatics.

Bob Medlar, Rare Coins. 4114 Ave., "Q," Lubbock, Texas 79412 (806-747-3456)
    General numismatics.

El Paso Coin Co., Renato Ruiz. Box "Q," El Paso, Texas 79901 (915-542-0242)
    General numismatics.

VERMONT

Myles Brown. Box 28, Burlington, Vt. 05401 (802-862-0115)
    General numismatics.

VIRGINIA

Midas Coin Centers, Col. Jay Jaynes. 5117 Backlick Rd., Annandale, Va. 22003 (703-256-2708)
General numismatics.

Steve Ruddel, Ltd. Box 1261, Springfield, Va. 22151 (703-941-9171)
General numismatics.

Falcon Coins. 1822 Horseback Trail, Vienna, Va. 22180 (703-938-3714)
General numismatics, silver bar specialist.

Dominion Coin Corp., Jerry Weinstein. Box 6-T, 517 E. Broad St., Richmond, Va. 23217
General numismatics.

Thalhimer Bros., Inc. (Coin Dept.), Richmond, Va. 23219 (703-653-4211, Ext. 526)
General numismatics and supplies.

Rocky's Coin Shop, R. W. Ward, Jr. 2926 W. Cary St., Richmond, Va. 23221 (703-353-3327)
General numismatics.

UTAH

Norman Shultz. Box 746A, Salt Lake City, Utah 84110
General numismatics.

WASHINGTON

Rare Coin Galleries of Seattle, Inc. Gene L. Henry. 1416 3rd Ave., Seattle, Wash. 98101 (206-624-4440)
General numismatics.

Liberty Coin Shop, Martin D. Levy. 114 Pike St., Seattle, Wash. 98101 (206-623-4088)
General numismatics.

June and Larry Hannick. 316 Virginia, Seattle, Wash. 98101 (206-622-0247)
General numismatics.

The Bon Marche (Coin Dept.), 4th & Pine Sts., Seattle, Wash. 98111 (206-624-1234)
General numismatics, supplies.

WISCONSIN

Gimbels (Coin Dept.), 101 W. Wisconsin Ave., Milwaukee, Wisc. 53201 (414-276-7050, Ext. 553)
General numismatics, supplies.

Fred Voecks. 227 E. College Ave., Appleton, Wisc. (414-733-4366)
General numismatics.